LOOK NO FURTHER

LOOK
NO
FURTHER

By RICHARD T. HOUGEN

ILLUSTRATIONS BY **ROBERT D. BIGELOW**

✛

ABINGDON PRESS

NEW YORK   NASHVILLE

LOOK NO FURTHER

Copyright © 1951, 1953, 1955 by Richard T. Hougen

PRINTED AND BOUND BY THE PARTHENON PRESS,
AT NASHVILLE, TENNESSEE, UNITED STATES OF AMERICA

TO MARY AND DONA CLARE

Goûtez les plaisirs de la table!

ACKNOWLEDGMENT

GRATEFUL THANKS TO MY FRIENDS WHO HAVE
ASSISTED ME IN PREPARING THIS MANUSCRIPT.

PREFACE

People who love to cook and people who love to eat are always looking for new recipes. For fifteen years, privately and professionally, I have been working with foods.

Through the years friends and acquaintances have asked me for my special recipes. This book contains these and also a selection of favorite ones from our family cookbook. Here too, you will find the popular recipes of our Boone Tavern kitchen.

I believe that the secret of good cooking is a combination of simplicity in procedure, accurate measurements, and the use of plenty of eggs, milk, butter, and cream. Although it is helpful to be enthusiastic about cooking it is by no means a necessity. There are those of us who love to cook and there are those of us who have to cook. But even the most unskillful cook can in most cases achieve wonders if he has good recipes. Here are 210.

It is my wish and plan that this book will be for each reader a handbook for the perfect finished food. This is a selection of specialties of the house rather than a collection of all types of foods. LOOK NO FURTHER is a cookbook designed for your cooking and eating pleasure.

Richard T. Hougen

CONTENTS

1.

BREADS

Who can think of Kentucky and not remember those tasty cornmeal dishes? Can you resist a second helping of Southern Spoon Bread, piping hot Spoon Cakes just turned from the griddle, and the popular Boone Tavern Cornsticks? Serve hot breads "hot" and sliced breads cold; plan a variety and bake plenty for all.

ALMOND BUNS

1 CAKE OF COMPRESSED YEAST
1/4 CUP WATER
1 TABLESPOON SUGAR
1 CUP SCALDED MILK
1 CUP FLOUR
2 EGG YOLKS
1/4 CUP MELTED BUTTER
1/4 CUP SUGAR
1 TEASPOON SALT
1/2 LB. CHOPPED BLANCHED ALMONDS, 1/4 CUP FINELY CHOPPED TO BE USED FOR THE TOP OF THE BUNS.
3 CUPS FLOUR

1. DISSOLVE YEAST WITH WATER AND SUGAR.
2. SCALD MILK. WHEN TEPID ADD YEAST MIXTURE.
3. ADD 1 CUP FLOUR AND MIX WELL. SET IN A WARM PLACE TO RISE AND BECOME LIGHT.
4. ADD REMAINING INGREDIENTS. MIX WELL. THE 3 CUPS OF FLOUR SHOULD BE ENOUGH TO MAKE A STIFF DOUGH.
5. ALLOW TO RISE DOUBLING IN BULK.
6. SHAPE INTO SMALL ROUNDS 1½ INCHES APART AND PLACE IN WELL GREASED PANS.
7. BRUSH TOPS WITH THE YOLK OF 1 EGG MIXED WITH 1 TABLESPOON OF MILK. SPRINKLE WITH CHOPPED ALMONDS.
8. ALLOW THE BUNS TO RISE UNTIL LIGHT. BAKE AT 350° F. FOR 20 TO 30 MINUTES.

2.

BOONE TAVERN CORNSTICKS

2 CUPS WHITE CORNMEAL
1/2 CUP FLOUR
2 EGGS, WELL BEATEN
1 TEASPOON BAKING
   POWDER
1/2 TEASPOON BAKING SODA
2 CUPS BUTTERMILK
1/2 TEASPOON SALT
4 TABLESPOONS MELTED
   LARD

1. SIFT FLOUR, CORNMEAL, SALT AND BAKING POWDER
   TOGETHER.
2. MIX SODA WITH BUTTERMILK. ADD TO DRY INGREDIENTS
   BEAT WELL.
3. ADD EGGS AND BEAT.
4. ADD LARD. MIX WELL.
5. POUR INTO WELL GREASED, SMOKING HOT, CORNSTICK
   PANS ON TOP OF STOVE. FILL PANS TO LEVEL.
6. PLACE ON LOWER SHELF OF OVEN AT 450° TO 500° F. FOR
   EIGHT MINUTES. MOVE TO UPPER SHELF AND BAKE 5 to
   10 MINUTES LONGER.

IT IS IMPORTANT TO HEAT WELL GREASED CORNSTICK
PANS TO SMOKING HOT ON TOP OF STOVE BEFORE
POURING IN YOUR BATTER. THIS RECIPE WILL MAKE ONE
DOZEN LARGE CORNSTICKS.

3.

CHERRY PECAN BREAD

1 4 OUNCE BOTTLE OF
MARASCHINO CHERRIES
1 EGG
1 CUP SUGAR
2 TABLESPOONS MELTED
BUTTER
3 TEASPOONS BAKING
POWDER
2 CUPS SIFTED FLOUR
1/4 TEASPOON BAKING SODA
3/4 TEASPOON SALT
1/4 CUP CHERRY JUICE
1/4 CUP EACH, ORANGE
JUICE AND WATER
1 CUP CHOPPED PECANS

1. BEAT THE EGG
2. ADD THE CHOPPED CHERRIES, WELL DRAINED.
3. STIR IN THE SUGAR AND MELTED BUTTER.
4. ADD CHERRY, ORANGE JUICE AND WATER.
5. SIFT TOGETHER FLOUR, BAKING POWDER, SODA AND
    SALT. ADD THESE AND BEAT WELL.
6. ADD CHOPPED NUTS.
7. PUT IN GREASED LOAF PAN 4$1/2$x8$1/2$" AND BAKE AT 350° F.
    FOR 1 HOUR.

4.

COFFEE CAKE, QUICK AND EASY

1 EGG
1 CUP BUTTERMILK
½ TEASPOON SODA
¾ CUP SUGAR
½ CUP BUTTER
2 TEASPOONS BAKING POWDER
2 CUPS FLOUR
½ TEASPOON SALT
½ CUP SUGAR MIXED WITH
¾ TEASPOON CINNAMON

1. CREAM SUGAR AND BUTTER. ADD BEATEN EGG.
2. SIFT FLOUR, SALT AND BAKING POWDER. ADD ALTERNATELY WITH THE BUTTERMILK MIXED WITH THE SODA.
3. THIS IS A THICK DOUGH. MIX WELL AND PLACE IN 2 BUTTERED PIE TINS. SPRINKLE TOPS WITH CINNAMON SUGAR.
4. BAKE AT 375° F. FOR 30 MINUTES. SERVE WARM.

USE SIFTED WHOLE WHEAT FLOUR AND BROWN SUGAR FOR A TASTY VARIATION.

DINNER ROLLS

2 EGGS
1 CUP SCALDED MILK
1/4 CUP BUTTER MELTED IN
   HOT MILK
1/4 CUP SUGAR
1 TEASPOON SALT
4 1/2 TO 5 CUPS FLOUR
1 COMPRESSED YEAST CAKE

1. SCALD MILK AND DISSOLVE BUTTER.
2. ADD SUGAR AND SALT. ALLOW TO COOL UNTIL TEPID.
3. ADD YEAST BY CRUMBLING INTO THE LIQUID, STIR TO DISSOLVE. ADD BEATEN EGGS AND FLOUR. STIR WELL.
4. PLACE IN A GREASED PAN, COVER AND SET IN A WARM PLACE TO RISE.
5. PUNCH DOUGH DOWN AND ALLOW TO RISE AGAIN.
6. ROLL OUT TO 1/2 INCH THICKNESS ON FLOURED PASTRY BOARD AND CUT INTO ROUNDS. PLACE THESE IN GREASED PAN AND ALLOW TO RISE.
7. BAKE FOR 12 TO 20 MINUTES AT 400° F.

A VARIETY OF SHAPES OTHER THAN ROUNDS MAY BE PERFECTED AND DIRECTED BY THE BAKER.

3 DOZEN ROLLS.

6.

GOOD SOUTHERN BISCUITS

2 CUPS SIFTED FLOUR
¾ TEASPOON SALT
1 TABLESPOON BAKING POWDER
¼ CUP LARD
1 CUP BUTTERMILK
¼ TEASPOON BAKING SODA

1. SIFT FLOUR, SALT, AND BAKING POWDER.
2. WORK IN LARD WITH FINGERTIPS.
3. MIX THE BAKING SODA WITH THE BUTTERMILK AND ADD TO THE FLOUR MIXTURE. BLEND LIGHTLY.
4. TOSS ON A HEAVILY FLOURED PASTRY BOARD AND KNEAD UNTIL SOFT AND SPONGY.
5. ROLL LIGHTLY TO ½ INCH THICKNESS AND CUT INTO ROUNDS.
6. PLACE ON WELL BUTTERED PAN. BAKE AT 450° TO 500° F. FOR 10 TO 12 MINUTES.

2 DOZEN BISCUITS.

GRIDDLE CAKES

2 CUPS FLOUR
1/4 CUP SUGAR
1/2 TEASPOON SALT
1 1/2 TEASPOON BAKING
POWDER
2 EGGS
1 1/2 CUPS MILK
4 TABLESPOONS BUTTER

1. SIFT THE FIRST FOUR INGREDIENTS.
2. BEAT EGGS WELL, ADD THE MILK.
3. MIX THE LIQUID WITH THE DRY INGREDIENTS.
4. ADD THE MELTED BUTTER AND MIX WELL.
5. BAKE ON A HOT PANCAKE GRIDDLE.

YOU MAY TEST THE TEMPERATURE OF THE GRIDDLE BY SPRINKLING A FEW DROPS OF WATER ON THE GRIDDLE. IF THE DROPS SEEM TO DANCE ABOUT AND EVAPORATE THE GRIDDLE IS THE CORRECT TEMPERATURE.

VARIATIONS FOR SUPPER DISHES:

1. BAKE THE CAKES ON ONE SIDE, SPRINKLE THE TOPS WITH TOASTED SHAVED BRAZIL NUTS OR ALMONDS AND TURN CAKE TO BAKE THE NUTTED SIDE.
2. SPREAD BAKED CAKES WITH TART APPLE SAUCE AND SPRINKLE THE TOP WITH POWDERED SUGAR.
3. BAKE THE CAKES ON ONE SIDE AND SPRINKLE THE TOPS WITH FRESH OR DRAINED FROZEN BLUEBERRIES. USE ONE TABLESPOONFUL BERRIES PER CAKE. TURN THE CAKE AND BAKE THE BLUEBERRIED SIDE.

SERVE ALL THE CAKES WITH BEATEN BUTTER OR WITH ORANGE, LEMON OR MAPLE BUTTER (RECIPES IN COOK-BOOK) AND HOT SYRUP.

8.

KOLACKY

2 CAKES COMPRESSED
YEAST
2½ CUPS MILK
¾ CUP SUGAR
2 EGGS
½ CUP BUTTER
5 TO 6 CUPS FLOUR
1 TEASPOON SALT

1. SCALD THE MILK, ADD BUTTER AND STIR TO DISSOLVE.
2. ALLOW THIS TO COOL UNTIL TEPID, THEN ADD THE YEAST BY CRUMBLING INTO THE MILK. STIR TO DISSOLVE.
3. ADD 2 CUPS OF THE SIFTED FLOUR, BEAT IN 1 EGG, SALT AND SUGAR. ADD 2 MORE CUPS OF FLOUR AND BEAT IN THE SECOND EGG. ADD 1 TO 3 CUPS OF FLOUR WHICH SHOULD MAKE A MEDIUM SOFT DOUGH.
4. PLACE ON A FLOURED PASTRY BOARD AND KNEAD WELL.
5. PLACE IN A GREASED BOWL, COVER AND SET IN A WARM PLACE TO RISE.
6. WHEN THE DOUGH HAS DOUBLED IN BULK PLACE ON A FLOURED PASTRY BOARD AND ROLL OUT ½ INCH THICK.
7. CUT INTO ROUNDS USING THE TOP OF A SMALL JUICE SIZE GLASS. PLACE ON A GREASED BAKING SHEET.
8. BRUSH OVER EACH ROUND WITH A MIXTURE MADE BY BEATING ONE EGG WITH ¼ CUP CREAM.
9. PRESS THE CENTERS DOWN OF EACH ROUND BY USING THE FOUR FINGERS (THUMB AND INDEX FINGER OF EACH HAND). THIS ENABLES YOU TO PRESS A CIRCLE DOWN LEAVING AN EDGE AROUND FOR ½ INCH.
10. THE CENTERS ARE THEN FILLED WITH AN ASSORTMENT OF KOLACKY FILLINGS.
11. ALLOW THE DOUGH TO RISE AND THEN BAKE AT 375° F. FOR 15 TO 20 MINUTES.
12. SERVE HOT HEAVILY DUSTED WITH CONFECTIONERS SUGAR. THE SUGAR IS SIFTED ONTO THE BUNS.

KOLACKY FILLINGS

PRUNE FILLING

½ LB. PRUNES
2 CUPS WATER
SUGAR
2 THIN SLICES OF ORANGE
2 SLICES OF LEMON

1. WASH THE PRUNES WELL AND COVER WITH 2 CUPS OF HOT WATER. ALLOW TO SOAK FOR 2 HOURS.
2. COOK UNTIL SOFT IN THE SAME WATER WITH ORANGE AND LEMON.
3. SWEETEN TO TASTE.
4. ALLOW TO COOL AND PIT THE PRUNES. THEY ARE THEN READY TO FILL THE BUNS. HAVE THE PRUNES MOIST.

APRICOT FILLING

USE THE SAME METHOD AS FOR THE PRUNES OMITTING THE ORANGE AND LEMON SLICES.

10.

COTTAGE CHEESE FILLING

$1/2$ TEASPOON FRESHLY
GRATED NUTMEG
1 CUP COTTAGE CHEESE
1 BEATEN EGG
$1/2$ CUP SUGAR

1. MIX ALL INGREDIENTS TOGETHER AND FILL THE CENTERS OF THE BUNS.

POPPY SEED FILLING

$1/2$ CUP POPPY SEEDS
$1/2$ CUP SUGAR
$1/4$ CUP WATER

1. BOIL SUGAR AND WATER TO A SYRUP.
2. STIR IN THE POPPY SEEDS AND FILL THE BUNS.

THIS IS NOT THE METHOD FOR THE BOHEMIAN PREPARATION OF THE POPPY SEED FILLING.

ANY OF THE THREE FILLINGS WILL BE SUFFICIENT TO FILL SEVEN DOZEN KOLACKY.

II.

PINEAPPLE MUFFINS

1/2 CUP SUGAR
1/4 CUP BUTTER
2 CUPS FLOUR, SIFT
BEFORE MEASURING
1 EGG
2 TEASPOONS BAKING
POWDER
1/8 TEASPOON BAKING
SODA
1 9 OUNCE CAN CRUSHED
PINEAPPLE
1/2 TEASPOON SALT

1. CREAM SUGAR AND BUTTER, ADD EGG AND BEAT WELL.
2. SIFT FLOUR, BAKING POWDER, SODA AND SALT.
3. ADD PINEAPPLE AND JUICE FROM CAN WITH FLOUR MIXTURE, TO THE BUTTER MIXTURE. BEAT WELL.
4. FILL SMALL MUFFIN TINS TWO-THIRDS FULL WITH BATTER.
5. BAKE AT 375° F FOR 25 MINUTES.

YIELD: 20 to 24 SMALL MUFFINS
VARIATIONS:

A. ORANGE MUFFINS
USE ABOVE RECIPE REPLACING THE PINEAPPLE AND JUICE WITH 1/2 CUP ORANGE JUICE AND GRATED RIND OF ONE ORANGE.

B. BLUEBERRY MUFFINS
USE RECIPE FOR ORANGE MUFFINS OMITTING THE ORANGE RIND AND ADDING ONE CUP FRESH OR DRAINED FROZEN BLUEBERRIES

C. NUT MUFFINS
USE ABOVE RECIPE SUBSTITUTING 1 CUP MILK AND 3/4 CUP CHOPPED PECANS FOR THE CRUSHED PINEAPPLE AND JUICE.

12.

POTATO MUFFINS

1 CAKE COMPRESSED YEAST
1 CUP WARM MILK
2 TABLESPOONS SUGAR
1 CUP MASHED POTATOES
1 TEASPOON BUTTER
1 TABLESPOON LARD
2 EGGS
1/2 TEASPOON SALT
1 QUART FLOUR

1. ADD THE BEATEN EGGS TO THE COOL MASHED POTA-
   TOES.
2. ADD WARM MILK IN WHICH YEAST, BUTTER, LARD, SALT
   AND SUGAR HAVE BEEN DISSOLVED.
3. STIR IN THE SIFTED FLOUR TO MAKE A FAIRLY STIFF
   DOUGH.
4. PLACE ON A BOARD AND KNEAD ONLY TO SMOOTH THE
   DOUGH. DO NOT ADD MORE FLOUR. YOU MAY RETAIN
   SOME OF THE FLOUR TO WORK INTO THE DOUGH ON
   THE BOARD. PLACE THE DOUGH IN A WELL GREASED
   BOWL AND SET TO RISE IN A WARM PLACE.
5. AFTER THE DOUGH HAS DOUBLED IN BULK MAKE INTO
   ROLLS. TAKE A PORTION OF THE DOUGH ONTO THE
   FLOURED BOARD AND ROLL OUT 1/2 INCH THICK. CUT
   INTO ROUNDS OR SIMPLY PINCH OFF SMALL BITS OF THE
   DOUGH SHAPING INTO SMALL BALLS AND PLACE THREE
   IN EACH CUP OF A GREASED MUFFIN PAN. BRUSH TOPS
   OF THE ROLLS WITH ONE BEATEN EGG YOLK MIXED WITH
   2 TABLESPOONS MILK.
6. ALLOW ROLLS TO DOUBLE IN SIZE AND THEN BAKE FOR
   12 TO 15 MINUTES AT 425° F.
   THESE ROLLS KEEP FRESH DUE TO THE MOISTURE OF THE
   POTATOES. IT IS A VERY LIGHT AND DELICIOUS ROLL.

13.

PRUNE AND BLACK WALNUT BREAD

1 CUP PRUNES
1/2 CUP PRUNE JUICE
1/4 CUP ORANGE JUICE
1 EGG
1 CUP SUGAR
2 TABLESPOONS MELTED BUTTER
3 TEASPOONS BAKING POWDER
2 CUPS SIFTED FLOUR
1/4 TEASPOON BAKING SODA
3/4 TEASPOON SALT
1 CUP BLACK WALNUT MEATS (CUT IN PIECES)

1. SOAK PRUNES FOR 1 HOUR.
2. DRAIN PRUNES WELL AND CUT IN SMALL PIECES.
3. BEAT EGG AND STIR IN SUGAR AND PRUNES.
4. ADD MELTED BUTTER.
5. SIFT FLOUR, BAKING POWDER, BAKING SODA AND SALT ADD TO THE MIXTURE ALTERNATELY WITH PRUNE AND ORANGE JUICE.
   MIX WELL.
6. ADD THE CHOPPED NUT MEATS.
7. PLACE IN GREASED LOAF TIN AND BAKE IN 350° F. OVEN FOR ABOUT 1 HOUR.

THIS RECIPE MAKES ONE LOAF OF BREAD.

14.

QUICK PECAN ROLLS

                    2 CUPS OF FLOUR
                    4 TEASPOONS BAKING
                      POWDER
                  2/3 TEASPOON SALT
                    4 TABLESPOONS
                      SHORTENING
                  2/3 CUP MILK
                    3 TABLESPOONS BUTTER
                    1 CUP BROWN SUGAR
                    1 CUP CUT PECANS
                    1 CUP BROWN SUGAR
                  1/2 CUP BUTTER

1. SIFT FLOUR, SALT AND BAKING POWDER.
2. MIX IN THE SHORTENING BY RUBBING IN WITH THE FIN-
    GERS. ADD 2/3 CUP MILK.
3. FORM A BALL AND ROLL OUT ON A FLOURED PASTRY
    BOARD TO 1/2 INCH THICK.
4. BLEND THE 3 TABLESPOONS BUTTER WITH 1 CUP BROWN
    SUGAR AND SPREAD OVER THE ROLLED DOUGH.
5. ROLL THE DOUGH AS FOR JELLY ROLL.
6. BLEND THE 1/2 CUP OF BUTTER WITH THE CUP OF BROWN
    SUGAR. PLACE A TEASPOON OF THIS MIXTURE IN THE
    BOTTOM OF EACH CUP OF A WELL GREASED MUFFIN
    PAN. SPRINKLE WITH A FEW PECANS AND PLACE IN A 1 1/2
    INCH SLICE OF THE DOUGH CUT FROM THE ROLL WITH
    THE CUT SIDE DOWN ON THE PECANS.
7. BAKE IN A QUICK OVEN 375° F. FOR 20 MINUTES.

THIS RECIPE WILL MAKE THREE DOZEN SMALL ROLLS OR
20 MEDIUM LARGE ROLLS. ALLOW THE ROLLS TO COOL
SOMEWHAT BEFORE REMOVING FROM THE PAN. THIS
WILL PERMIT CARAMELIZED SUGAR TO ADHERE TO THE
ROLL.

15.

SOUTHERN SPOON BREAD

3 CUPS MILK
1¼ CUPS CORNMEAL
3 EGGS
2 TABLESPOONS BUTTER
1¾ TEASPOONS BAKING POWDER
1 TEASPOON SALT

1. STIR MEAL INTO RAPIDLY BOILING MILK. COOK UNTIL VERY THICK, STIRRING CONSTANTLY, TO PREVENT SCORCHING.
2. REMOVE FROM FIRE AND ALLOW TO COOL. THE MIXTURE WILL BE COLD AND VERY STIFF.
3. ADD WELL BEATEN EGG, SALT, BAKING POWDER AND MELTED BUTTER. BEAT WITH ELECTRIC BEATER FOR 15 MINUTES. IF HAND BEATING IS USED BREAK THE HARDENED COOKED MEAL INTO THE BEATEN EGGS IN SMALL AMOUNTS UNTIL ALL IS WELL MIXED. THEN BEAT THOROUGHLY FOR 10 MINUTES USING A WOODEN SPOON.
4. POUR INTO WELL GREASED CASSEROLE. BAKE FOR 30 MINUTES AT 375° F. SERVE FROM CASSEROLE BY SPOONFULS.

THIS IS THE SPOON BREAD FOR WHICH BOONE TAVERN IS SO FAMOUS. BE SURE TO USE WHITE CORNMEAL FOR THE TRUE SOUTHERN BREAD.

SPOON CAKES

1 CUP BUTTERMILK
1½ CUPS WHITE CORNMEAL
4 EGGS
¼ TEASPOON BAKING SODA
½ TEASPOON BAKING
POWDER
4 TABLESPOONS MELTED
BUTTER
¼ CUP WATER
½ TEASPOON SALT

1. SIFT DRY INGREDIENTS.
2. ADD BUTTERMILK AND WATER. BEAT. ADD BEATEN EGGS. BEAT.
3. ADD MELTED BUTTER LAST AND BEAT ALL TOGETHER.
4. DROP BY SPOONFULS ONTO A HISSING HOT GRIDDLE WHICH HAS BEEN GREASED BEFORE COOKING EACH CAKE. ONE MAY USE A LARGE SKILLET IF DESIRED.
5. SERVE PIPING HOT FROM THE GRIDDLE.

THESE SPOON CAKES ARE ONE OF THE FAVORITE BOONE TAVERN HOT BREADS. THEY ARE CUT IN HALF AND EATEN BY BUTTERING A BITE AND HOLDING THE CAKE IN YOUR FINGERS. FOR ME . . . GIVE ME SPOON CAKES, HONEY AND COFFEE.

17.

ORANGE BUTTER TOAST

½ CUP BUTTER, ALLOW TO SOFTEN AT ROOM TEMPERATURE
1 CUP SIFTED CONFECTIONERS SUGAR
GRATED RIND AND JUICE OF ONE ORANGE

1. BEAT THE BUTTER WITH AN ELECTRIC EGG BEATER OR BY HAND. WHEN IT IS OF THE CONSISTENCY OF WHIPPED CREAM ADD THE ORANGE JUICE AND THE RIND. WHIP ALL TOGETHER AGAIN. THIS WILL CAUSE THE BUTTER TO CURD.
2. ADD THE CONFECTIONERS SUGAR AND WHIP AGAIN UNTIL LIGHT. THE AMOUNT OF ORANGE JUICE USED WILL VARY THE AMOUNT OF CONFECTIONERS SUGAR REQUIRED. SUGGEST USING TART ORANGES.

THIS BUTTER IS USED ON TOAST FOR TEA OR FOR A SALAD ACCOMPANIMENT. IT IS LIKEWISE DESIRABLE FOR USE ON WAFFLES OR PAN CAKES. THE BUTTER WILL KEEP IN THE REFRIGERATOR AND CAN BE SOFTENED AND REWHIPPED WHEN NEEDED.

18.

LEMON BUTTER

USE THE RECIPE FOR ORANGE BUTTER SUBSTITUTING LEMON
JUICE FOR THE ORANGE JUICE. HALF OF THE JUICE OF ONE
LEMON IS SUFFICIENT.

MAPLE BUTTER

USE RECIPE FOR ORANGE BUTTER SUBSTITUTING 2 TEA-
SPOONS OF MAPLE EXTRACT OR $1/2$ CUP OF PURE MAPLE
SYRUP FOR THE ORANGE JUICE.

NUTTED SPREAD ON
WHOLE WHEAT WHITE

$1/2$ CUP CHOPPED WALNUTS
$1/2$ CUP CHOPPED PECANS
$1/2$ CUP RAISINS
$1/2$ CUP HONEY
WHOLE WHEAT AND
WHITE BREAD

1. MIX NUTS, RAISINS AND HONEY TOGETHER.
2. SPREAD ON A BUTTERED PIECE OF WHOLE WHEAT
   BREAD. COMPLETE THE SANDWICH WITH A BUTTERED
   SLICE OF WHITE BREAD.
3. CUT THE SANDWICH IN TRIANGLES AND SERVE WITH A
   SPICED CRABAPPLE.

19.

SNAPPY CHEESE SPREAD

3 LB. CHEDDAR CHEESE
1½ LB. CREAM CHEESE
½ LB. BUTTER
MIX THE FOLLOWING INGRE-
DIENTS TOGETHER:
¼ CUP CHICKEN BROTH
¼ CUP PAPRIKA
1 TEASPOON DRY MUSTARD
1 TEASPOON WORCESTER
SAUCE
1 TEASPOON CATSUP
¼ TEASPOON SALT
¼ TEASPOON PEPPER

1. GRIND THE FIRST THREE ITEMS. THEN MIX THE BROTH IN WHICH THE OTHER ITEMS HAVE BEEN MIXED INTO THE GROUND MIXTURE.
2. BLEND ALL TOGETHER WITH AN ELECTRIC BEATER.
3. PLACE IN AN EARTHENWARE JAR AND COVER WITH WAX PAPER. THIS MAY BE KEPT IN THE REFRIGERATOR FOR SOMETIME.

THIS SPREAD IS IDEAL FOR TOASTED CHEESE SANDWICHES. SPREAD TOAST WITH THIS MIXTURE AND PLACE UNDER THE BROILER. THIS MAY ALSO BE USED AS A SANDWICH FILLER, FOR MAKING SMALL CHEESE APPLES OR CARROTS AS GARNITURES, ETC. FOR A SMALL FAMILY I WOULD SUGGEST MAKING ONLY HALF THE ABOVE AT ONE TIME.

20.

TOASTED ALMOND SPREAD

1 CUP GROUND TOASTED
ALMONDS
1/2 CUP BUTTER
1/4 CUP MAYONNAISE
3 OUNCES CREAM CHEESE

1. MIX ALL TOGETHER BY USING AN ELECTRIC BEATER.
2. THIS IS EXCELLENT FOR USE ON TOAST AND FOR GRILL-
ING, SPREAD OVER ENGLISH MUFFINS, WITH HOT BRAN
MUFFINS, OR SPREAD OVER PIECES OF SPONGE CAKE.
BROIL AND SERVE FOR TEA (NOTHING TASTIER).

❖

22.

NOTES

23.

NOTES

24.

NOTES

25.

2.

CAKES

The following recipes give you a light delicate texture cake. Always use rich dairy products. Unless otherwise specified, use an all purpose flour. Most of these are simple to combine yet the more elaborate ones receive noble praise from the consumers. It would be difficult to select a favorite from this group for I believe these are really special cakes.

Please notice the icing follows each cake recipe except where Boiled Icing is called for.

BANBURY CROSS CAKE

I TEASPOON SODA
I CUP CURRANTS
2 CUPS HOT WATER
I CUP SUGAR
1/3 CUP BUTTER
I EGG
1¾ CUPS SIFTED FLOUR
I TEASPOON MACE
I TEASPOON NUTMEG
½ TEASPOON SALT

1. BOIL THE CURRANTS AND WATER FOR 15 MINUTES. ADD THE BAKING SODA AND MIX WELL. ALLOW MIXTURE TO COOL.
2. CREAM THE SUGAR AND BUTTER.
3. ADD THE EGG AND BEAT TOGETHER WELL.
4. SIFT THE FLOUR WITH THE SPICES AND SALT.
5. ADD THE FLOUR MIXTURE TO THE CREAMED MIXTURE WITH THE CURRANTS. BEAT ALL TOGETHER WELL.
6. BAKE IN A WELL GREASED 7½ X 11 INCH PAN AT 350° F. FOR 45 TO 50 MINUTES.
7. ALLOW CAKE TO COOL AND FROST WITH CARAMEL ICING GIVEN ON PAGE 29.

28.

CARAMEL ICING

1 1/2 CUPS BROWN SUGAR
PINCH SALT
1/3 CUP BUTTERMILK
2 TABLESPOONS BUTTER

1. MIX THE SUGAR, MILK AND SALT. PLACE ON MEDIUM HEAT TO BOIL. STIR WELL TO DISSOLVE THE SUGAR CRYSTALS.
2. TEST BY DROPPING ABOUT A TEASPOONFUL OF THE HOT SYRUP IN A SAUCER OF COLD WATER. WHEN THE SYRUP FORMS A SOFT YET WELL SHAPED BALL IN THE COLD WATER REMOVE FROM THE STOVE AND ADD THE BUTTER.
3. ALLOW THE ICING TO STAND UNTIL COLD THEN HAND BEAT UNTIL IT IS OF THE RIGHT CONSISTENCY TO SPREAD ON THE CAKE. BEATING TIME IS ABOUT 10 TO 12 MINUTES.

BLUEBERRY CUP CAKES

1½ CUPS FLOUR
1½ TEASPOONS BAKING
POWDER
½ CUP BUTTER
1 CUP SUGAR
2 UNBEATEN EGGS
½ CUP MILK
1 TEASPOON LEMON
EXTRACT
1 CUP DRAINED CANNED
BLUEBERRIES

1. CREAM BUTTER, ADD SUGAR GRADUALLY AND CREAM UNTIL FLUFFY.
2. ADD EGGS ONE AT A TIME AND BEAT WELL.
3. ADD FLOUR AND BAKING POWDER, WHICH HAS BEEN SIFTED THREE TIMES, ALTERNATELY WITH THE MILK AND FLAVORING, BEGINNING AND ENDING WITH THE FLOUR MIXTURE. BEAT WELL.
4. ADD BLUEBERRIES AND FOLD THEM IN.
5. FILL WELL GREASED CUP CAKE PANS 2/3 FULL AND BAKE FOR 20 MINUTES AT 375° F.
6. COOL AND FROST WITH MAPLE PECAN FROSTING.
7. RECIPE FOR MAPLE PECAN FROSTING GIVEN ON PAGE 31.

MAPLE PECAN FROSTING

½ CUP MAPLE SYRUP
3 TABLESPOONS BUTTER
2¾ CUPS CONFECTIONERS
SUGAR
1/8 TEASPOON SALT
1 CUP CHOPPED PECANS
1 TABLESPOON CREAM

1. COOK THE SYRUP SLOWLY FOR 3 MINUTES. COOL.
2. CREAM BUTTER AND ADD THE SIFTED SUGAR GRADUALLY
ALTERNATELY WITH THE SYRUP. BEAT WELL ADDING
CREAM AND SALT.
3. WHIP ALL TOGETHER UNTIL LIGHT AND SPREAD ON TOP
OF THE CAKES. DUST TOPS WITH THE CHOPPED PECANS.

YIELD: 1 DOZEN OR MORE CUP CAKES DEPENDING ON SIZE
CUP CAKE PAN USED.

✙

BROILED SUGAR COCONUT CAKE

1 CUP BROWN SUGAR
½ CUP BUTTER
2 EGGS, WELL BEATEN
½ TEASPOON CLOVES
1 TEASPOON CINNAMON
2 CUPS WHOLE WHEAT
FLOUR
1 CUP PASTUERIZED
CREAM (SOUR)
1 TEASPOON BAKING SODA
½ CUP APPLE SAUCE
1 CUP RAISINS

1. CREAM THE BUTTER AND SUGAR.
2. ADD EGGS AND MIX WELL.
3. SIFT FLOUR AND SPICES.
4. MIX THE RAISINS INTO THE FLOUR MIXTURE TO SEPARATE THE PARTICLES.
5. MIX THE BAKING SODA WITH THE CREAM.
6. ADD THE FLOUR MIXTURE, CREAM, AND APPLE SAUCE TO THE CREAMED MIXTURE OF STEP NUMBER TWO. BEAT ALL TOGETHER TO MIX WELL.
7. BAKE IN A WELL GREASED 8 X 11 INCH PAN AT 350° F. FOR 30 MINUTES. DURING THIS BAKING PERIOD PREPARE THE ICING AS FOLLOWS ON PAGE 33:

¼ CUP BUTTER
¾ CUP BROWN SUGAR
1 CUP SHREDDED
COCONUT

A. MELT THE BUTTER AND ADD THE SUGAR AND COCO-NUT.
B. AFTER THE CAKE HAS BAKED THIRTY MINUTES REMOVE FROM OVEN BY PULLING OUT THE OVEN RACK ENOUGH TO PERMIT ROOM TO SPREAD THE ICING OVER THE CAKE.
C. RETURN CAKE TO OVEN AND TURN ON BROILER TOP ALLOWING THE ICING TO SIZZLE FOR ABOUT THREE MINUTES.

THIS EASILY MIXED AND ICED CAKE WITH ITS SPICY FRAGRANCE IS SO TEMPTING IT RARELY HAS TIME TO COOL BEFORE IT IS EATEN.

CHOCOLATE CAKE

1/4 CUP BUTTER
3/4 CUP SUGAR
2 BEATEN EGG YOLKS
2 OZ. MELTED CHOCOLATE
1 CUP FLOUR
1 TEASPOON SODA
2/3 CUP MILK
1/4 TEASPOON VANILLA
1 TEASPOON BAKING
POWDER

1. CREAM THE BUTTER AND SUGAR
2. ADD THE EGG YOLKS AND THE MELTED CHOCOLATE.
3. SIFT THE FLOUR WITH THE BAKING POWDER AND SODA.
4. ADD THE FLOUR ALTERNATELY WITH THE MILK, BEGIN AND END WITH A PORTION OF THE FLOUR.
5. ADD THE VANILLA AND BEAT WELL.
6. BAKE IN A WELL GREASED 8x8 INCH PAN FOR 30 MINUTES AT 350° F.
7. FROST WITH BOILED ICING.

✣

34.

DEVILS FOOD CAKE

1½ CUPS SUGAR
½ CUP BUTTER
3 EGGS
½ CUP COCOA MOISTENED WITH ½ CUP BOILING WATER
1 LEVEL TEASPOON SODA MIXED WITH ½ CUP BUT-TERMILK
2 CUPS (LEVEL) SIFTED FLOUR

1. CREAM BUTTER AND SUGAR WELL.
2. ADD EGGS AND BEAT WELL.
3. ADD SIFTED FLOUR, COCOA MELTED IN THE HOT WATER, SODA AND BUTTTERMILK. STIR ALL TOGETHER VIGOROUS-LY.
4. PLACE IN A 9x12 INCH PAN WELL GREASED AND BAKE FOR 50 MINUTES AT 350° F.
5. ALLOW TO COOL AND FROST WITH BOILED ICING.

✣

DOLLY VARDEN CAKE

3/4 CUP BUTTER
4 EGGS
1 1/2 CUPS MILK
1 1/2 CUPS SUGAR
3 CUPS FLOUR
3 1/2 TEASPOONS BAKING
POWDER

1. CREAM BUTTER AND SUGAR TOGETHER WELL.
2. ADD EGGS AND MIX WELL.
3. SIFT FLOUR BEFORE MEASURING AND THEN SIFT WITH THE BAKING POWDER INTO THE CAKE. ADD MILK ALTERNATING, BEGINNING AND ENDING WITH THE FLOUR.
4. SEPARATE THE BATTER INTO THREE PARTS. PUT ONE THIRD IN ONE LAYER FOR THE YELLOW LAYER, TO THE SECOND THIRD ADD 1/2 TEASPOON RED COLORING AND PLACE IN LAYER PAN. TO THE REMAINING THIRD ADD THE FOLLOWING INGREDIENTS:
1/2 CUP RAISINS
1/4 CUP CUT WALNUTS
1/4 TEASPOON CLOVES
1/4 TEASPOON CINNAMON
1 TEASPOON MOLASSES WITH 1/4 TEASPOON SODA
5. BAKE ALL THREE LAYERS FOR 30 MINUTES AT 350° F.
6. WHEN COOL FROST WITH BOILED ICING TO WHICH 1/2 CUP EACH OF CHOPPED WALNUTS AND GROUND RAISINS HAVE BEEN ADDED.

HUNTING CAKES

> 1 CUP SUGAR
> 1/2 CUP BUTTER
> 1 CUP SOUR CREAM
> 2 EGGS
> 1/2 TEASPOON CLOVES
> 1 TEASPOON SODA
> 1 TEASPOON CINNAMON
> 1 CUP RAISINS (CUT WITH
>   SCISSORS)
> 1/2 CUP WALNUTS
> 2 CUPS FLOUR, SIFTED
>   BEFORE MEASURING

1. CREAM BUTTER AND SUGAR.
2. ADD EGGS, BEAT WELL.
3. SIFT FLOUR, SPICES AND MIX IN THE CUT RAISINS AND CHOPPED NUTS. THIS WILL SEPARATE THE PARTICLES. MIX SODA WITH SOUR CREAM AND ADD ALTERNATELY WITH THE FLOUR MIXTURE. MIX WELL.
4. BAKE IN CUP CAKES AT 350° F. FOR 20 OR 30 MINUTES.
5. FROST EACH CAKE WITH BOILED ICING AND PLACE A HALF DATE ON TOP OF EACH CAKE.

✤

JAMAICA SPONGE

                    1 CUP SUGAR
                    1/4 CUP MILK
                    2 TABLESPOONS BUTTER
                    1 CUP FLOUR
                    1 TEASPOON BAKING
                      POWDER
                    3 EGGS
                    1/4 CUP MOLASSES
                    1/2 TEASPOON GINGER

1. BEAT EGGS WELL AND BEAT IN SUGAR.
2. SIFT FLOUR WITH BAKING POWDER AND GINGER 3 TIMES.
3. ADD FLOUR MIXTURE AND BEAT WELL.
4. HEAT MILK AND MOLASSES TO BOILING POINT. ADD BUTTER AND FOLD CAREFULLY INTO MIXTURE.
5. BAKE IN A GREASED PAN 10x10 INCHES AT 350° F. FOR 30 MINUTES.
6. ALLOW TO COOL AND FROST WITH BANANA WHIP. RECIPE FOR BANANA WHIP ON PAGE 39.

✤

BANANA WHIP

1 EGG YOLK
2 TABLESPOONS CREAM
2 CUPS SIFTED POWDERED
SUGAR
1½ TEASPOONS BANANA
EXTRACT
½ CUP MELTED BUTTER
1 CUP SHAVED BRAZIL NUTS

1. BEAT EGG YOLK, ADD CREAM AND BEAT WELL.
2. ADD ½ CUP OF XXXX SUGAR, BEAT WELL, ADD ANOTHER
½ CUP XXXX SUGAR, BEAT WELL, THEN ADD 1 CUP
XXXX SUGAR AND THE MELTED BUTTER, BEAT WELL.
3. ADD BANANA EXTRACT AND WHIP ALL TOGETHER UNTIL
THE CONSISTENCY OF WHIPPED CREAM.
4. SPREAD ON CAKE AND DUST TOP WELL WITH BRAZIL
NUTS.

✤

PISTACHIO NUT CAKE

        9 EGGS
      1/4 TEASPOON SALT
        1 TEASPOON CREAM OF
          TARTAR
    1 1/8 CUPS SUGAR
        4 TABLESPOONS ORANGE
          JUICE (FROZEN TYPE)
          GRATED RIND OF 1
          ORANGE
    1 1/8 CUPS CAKE FLOUR
          MEASURE AFTER SIFTING

1. BEAT THE EGG WHITES WITH THE SALT UNTIL FOAMY. ADD CREAM OF TARTAR AND BEAT UNTIL STIFF.
2. ADD 2/3 CUP SUGAR GRADUALLY, BEATING WELL AFTER EACH ADDITION OF THE SUGAR.
3. BEAT EGG YOLKS UNTIL VERY THICK. ADD REMAINING SUGAR AND BEAT WELL.
4. ADD ORANGE JUICE AND RIND TO THE EGG YOLKS AND MIX TOGETHER.
5. FOLD EGG YOLK MIXTURE INTO THE EGG WHITE MIXTURE.
6. SIFT FLOUR OVER THIS AND CAREFULLY FOLD TOGETHER.
7. POUR INTO A LARGE UNBUTTERED ANGEL FOOD TIN AND BAKE AT 300° F. FOR 1 HOUR.
8. ALLOW TO COOL INVERTED ON A CAKE RACK. REMOVE CAKE TO CAKE PLATE AND CUT IN THREE LAYERS.
9. FILL WITH THE FOLLOWING FILLING:

FILLING

¾ PINT WHIPPED CREAM
¾ CUP SUGAR
JUICE AND GRATED RIND
OF 1 ORANGE
1 TABLESPOON LEMON JUICE
4 TABLESPOONS FLOUR
1 EGG

1. BEAT EGG, ADD JUICE, RIND AND SUGAR. STIR IN SIFTED FLOUR.
2. COOK IN A DOUBLE BOILER UNTIL THICKENED.
3. ALLOW TO COOL AND FOLD IN WHIPPED CREAM.
4. SPREAD FILLING BETWEEN THE TWO LAYERS AND FROST WITH THE FOLLOWING ICING FOUND ON PAGE 42:

ICING, PISTACHIO NUT CAKE

1 EGG YOLK
3 CUPS CONFECTIONERS
SUGAR (SIFTED)
4 TABLESPOONS BUTTER
2 TABLESPOONS CREAM
2 TABLESPOONS ORANGE
JUICE
GRATED RIND OF 1
ORANGE
2 CUPS CHOPPED
PISTACHIO NUTS

1. MELT BUTTER AND ADD TO SUGAR. CREAM TOGETHER
AND ADD ORANGE JUICE, RIND AND CREAM. STIR IN
BEATEN EGG. BEAT WELL TO FORM A SMOOTH FROST-
ING.
2. FROST SIDES AND TOP OF CAKE.
3. SPRINKLE NUTS OVER TOP AND SIDES OF THE CAKE.
PRESS THEM SLIGHTLY INTO THE FROSTING.
4. PLACE CAKE IN THE REFRIGERATOR FOR 3 HOURS TO
CHILL WELL BEFORE SERVING.

THIS IS AN OUTSTANDING DESSERT FOR A SPECIAL DINNER
OR AN UNUSUAL PASTRY TO SERVE IN THE AFTERNOON
OR EVENING.

POTATO CAKE

2 CUPS SUGAR
1 CUP SHORTENING
4 EGGS
1 CUP MASHED POTATOES
1/2 TEASPOON VANILLA
1 TEASPOON CLOVES
1 TEASPOON CINNAMON
1/2 CUP MILK
1 CUP WALNUT MEATS
(CUT FINE)
2 CUPS FLOUR (SIFTED
BEFORE MEASURING)
2 TEASPOONS BAKING
POWDER
1/2 CUP DUTCH PROCESS
COCOA

1. CREAM SUGAR AND SHORTENING.
2. ADD BEATEN EGGS AND MIX WELL.
3. ADD POTATOES, VANILLA, CINNAMON, AND CLOVES. MIX WELL.
4. SIFT FLOUR, BAKING POWDER, AND COCOA TOGETHER, ADD ALTERNATELY WITH THE MILK, BEGINNING AND ENDING WITH THE FLOUR. ADD NUTS.
5. MIX WELL AND BAKE IN A GREASED SHEET CAKE PAN 9x10 INCHES AT 350° F. FOR 30 TO 40 MINUTES.
6. ALLOW TO COOL AND ICE WITH BOILED ICING. SEE PAGE 52.

THIS CAKE WILL STAY MOIST DUE TO THE POTATO CONTENT. IT IS MY FAVORITE CAKE.

43.

PRINCE OF WALES CAKE

1 CUP SUGAR
1/2 CUP BUTTER
2 EGGS, WELL BEATEN
1 TABLESPOON MOLASSES
1/2 CUP RAISINS
1/2 CUP DATES
2 CUPS ALL PURPOSE FLOUR
1/8 TEASPOON CINNAMON
1/8 TEASPOON CLOVES
1/8 TEASPOON NUTMEG
1/8 TEASPOON SALT
1 TEASPOON BAKING POWDER
1 CUP BUTTERMILK MIXED WITH 1 TEASPOON SODA

1. CREAM TOGETHER BUTTER AND SUGAR.
2. ADD EGGS AND MOLASSES. BEAT WELL.
3. ADD RAISINS AND DATES WHICH HAVE BEEN GROUND IN A FOOD CHOPPER. BEAT WELL.
4. SIFT AND MEASURE FLOUR. THEN ADD SPICES, SALT AND BAKING POWDER.
5. SIFT FLOUR AND SPICES INTO THE CREAMED MIXTURE ALTERNATING WITH BUTTERMILK AND SODA MIXTURE. REMEMBER TO BEGIN AND END WITH THE FLOUR. BEAT WELL.
6. BAKE IN TWO LAYER TINS WELL GREASED WITH BUTTER FOR 20 TO 25 MINUTES AT 350° F.
7. REMOVE FROM OVEN AND ALLOW TO COOL.
8. REMOVE CAKE FROM FIRST PAN AND PLACE ON CAKE PLATE. SPREAD WITH THE FOLLOWING FILLING:

FILLING

3 EGG YOLKS
1 CUP MILK
2½ TABLESPOONS FLOUR
1 CUP SUGAR
¼ CUP FINELY CHOPPED
WALNUTS
1 TEASPOON VANILLA

1. BEAT EGG YOLKS UNTIL LIGHT.
2. MIX FLOUR TO A SMOOTH PASTE WITH MILK.
3. BEAT IN SUGAR. COMBINE MIXTURES.
4. COOK IN A DOUBLE BOILER. STIR TO PREVENT LUMPING.
5. WHEN THICKENED (AFTER ABOUT 8 MINUTES OF COOK-
   ING) REMOVE FROM FIRE AND COOL. WHEN COOL ADD
   WALNUTS. THEN ADD VANILLA. SPREAD ON CAKE.
6. PLACE SECOND LAYER OF CAKE ON TOP OF THE FILLING.
7. ICE THE CAKE COMPLETELY WITH BOILED OR SEVEN
   MINUTE ICING.

❖

QUAKER CAKE

I WHOLE EGG
2 EGG YOLKS (WHITES MAY
BE USED FOR ICING)
I CUP SUGAR
1/2 CUP BUTTER
I CUP BUTTERMILK
I TEASPOON SODA
I TEASPOON CINNAMON
I TEASPOON BAKING
POWDER
I CUP RAISINS (CUT WITH
SCISSORS)
2 CUPS FLOUR

1. CREAM BUTTER AND SUGAR. ADD BEATEN EGG AND YOLKS.
2. SIFT FLOUR, BAKING POWDER AND CINNAMON. MIX IN THE RAISINS IN ORDER TO SEPARATE THE RAISIN PIECES.
3. MIX SODA WITH BUTTERMILK AND ADD ALTERNATELY WITH THE FLOUR, BEGIN AND END WITH THE FLOUR.
4. POUR INTO TWO WELL GREASED LAYER CAKE PANS.
5. BAKE FOR 20 TO 25 MINUTES AT 350° F.
6. WHEN COOL PUT LAYERS TOGETHER WITH THE FOLLOWING FILLING:

QUAKER CAKE FILLING

1½ TABLESPOONS FLOUR
½ CUP SUGAR
½ CUP WATER
½ CUP RAISINS (CUT)
2 LARGE BANANAS (SLICED THIN)
½ CUP BUTTER
½ CUP CHOPPED NUTS, USE WALNUTS OR PECANS

1. MIX FLOUR WITH THE SUGAR.
2. ADD WATER AND COOK IN A DOUBLE BOILER UNTIL THICKENED.
3. ADD RAISINS AND BANANAS. COOK WELL.
4. REMOVE FROM THE FIRE AND ADD BUTTER AND NUTS.
5. COOL SLIGHTLY AND SPREAD BETWEEN THE TWO LAYERS. ALSO SPREAD A LAYER OF FILLING ON TOP OF THE CAKE.
6. MAKE A RECIPE OF BOILED ICING AND FROST THE SIDES OF THE CAKE. DO NOT FROST OVER THE TOP.

✤

SUNSHINE CAKE

1 1/3 CUPS SUGAR
1/4 CUP WATER
WHITES OF 6 EGGS
1 LEVEL TEASPOON
CREAM OF TARTAR
1 TEASPOON VANILLA
6 BEATEN EGG YOLKS
1 CUP FLOUR, LESS 1 TEA-
SPOONFUL, SIFTED 5
TIMES
1/8 TEASPOON SALT

1. MOISTEN SUGAR WITH THE COLD WATER AND STIR WELL TO COMPLETELY DISSOLVE. PLACE ON FIRE AND LET BOIL UNTIL IT SPINS A LONG THREAD. IT IS A GOOD PLAN TO COVER THIS MIXTURE AT THE BEGINNING AND ALLOW THE STEAM TO DISSOLVE SUGAR CRYSTALS THAT MAY ADHERE TO THE SIDES OF THE PAN.
2. BEAT EGG WHITES AND WHEN FOAMY ADD CREAM OF TARTAR AND CONTINUE BEATING UNTIL THEY HOLD IN STIFF PEAKS.
3. POUR BOILING HOT SYRUP OVER THE EGG WHITES BY FOLDING METHOD.
4. FOLD IN BEATEN EGG YOLKS, SALT AND VANILLA.
5. FOLD IN SIFTED FLOUR.
6. BAKE IN AN UNGREASED ANGEL FOOD PAN FOR 50 MINUTES AT 325° F.
7. REMOVE FROM OVEN AND INVERT CAKE ON CAKE RACK.
8. WHEN COOL LOOSEN EDGES OF CAKE FROM SIDES OF PAN WITH A SHARP KNIFE. REMOVE CAKE TO CAKE PLATE.
9. FROST WITH BOILED ICING.

48.

TUMBLEWEED CAKE

        6 EGGS
        I CUP SUGAR
        I CUP PASTRY FLOUR
        I TABLESPOON LEMON
          JUICE
      ¾ TABLESPOON GRATED
          LEMON RIND
      ½ TEASPOON VANILLA
      ¼ TEASPOON SALT
        I LB. CHOPPED FINE
          PEANUTS OR ALMONDS

1. BEAT EGG WHITES UNTIL STIFF AND ADD HALF OF THE SUGAR BY FOLDING IN WITH LONG STROKES INCORPORATING AS MUCH AIR INTO THE MIXTURE AS POSSIBLE.
2. BEAT THE YOLKS UNTIL LEMON COLORED, ADD REMAINING SUGAR, LEMON RIND, JUICE, SALT AND VANILLA. BEAT VERY WELL.
3. FOLD THIS INTO THE EGG WHITES USING LONG, CAREFUL STROKES INCORPORATING AS MUCH AIR AS POSIBLE. FOLD IN FLOUR BY SAME METHOD.
4. PLACE IN AN 8x12 INCH PAN AND BAKE FOR 25 TO 50 MINUTES AT 325° F. DO NOT GREASE PAN.
5. ALLOW TO COOL INVERTING THE PAN ON A WIRE RACK.
6. CUT CAKE INTO 2 INCH SQUARES AND REMOVE FROM THE PAN ONTO A TOWEL.
7. FROST ON 6 SIDES. ROLL IN CHOPPED TOASTED PEANUTS OR ALMONDS.
8. FROSTING RECIPE ON PAGE 50.

FROSTING FOR TUMBLEWEED CAKE

3 CUPS SIFTED CONFECTION-
ERS SUGAR
1/2 CUP MELTED BUTTER
2 TABLESPOONS CREAM
1 TABLESPOON LEMON
JUICE

1. BLEND THE LEMON JUICE AND CREAM INTO THE SUGAR.
2. ADD THE BUTTER AND BEAT UNTIL LIGHT AND CREAMY.
3. FROST THE CUT PIECES OF CAKE ON ALL 6 SIDES. ROLL
IN CHOPPED ALMONDS OR SALTED PEANUTS. YOU WILL
NEED APPROXIMATELY 3/4 LB. OF CHOPPED NUTS.

WHITE CAKE

1/2 CUP BUTTER
1 CUP SUGAR
WHITES OF 3 EGGS
2/3 CUP MILK
2 CUPS PASTRY FLOUR,
SIFTED BEFORE MEASUR-
ING
2 1/2 TEASPOONS BAKING
POWDER
1 TEASPOON VANILLA

1. CREAM BUTTER AND SUGAR.
2. SIFT FLOUR WITH BAKING POWDER. ADD ALTERNATELY
WITH THE MILK, BEGINNING AND ENDING WITH FLOUR.
3. MIX IN VANILLA AND BEAT WELL.
4. ADD STIFFLY BEATEN EGG WHITES BY FOLDING INTO THE
CAKE.
5. BAKE IN A 9x9 INCH PAN AT 350° F. FOR 40 MINUTES.
6. ALLOW CAKE TO COOL AND FROST WITH ALMOND
TOFFEE CREAM.

50.

ALMOND TOFFEE CREAM

3 CUPS CONFECTIONERS
SUGAR
2 TABLESPOONS CREAM
1 TEASPOON ALMOND
EXTRACT
5 TEASPOONS COFFEE SYRUP
1/2 CUP MELTED BUTTER
1 CUP CHOPPED ALMONDS,
TOASTED

1. SIFT CONFECTIONERS SUGAR. ADD CREAM AND EXTRACT.
2. ADD 5 TEASPOONS COFFEE SYRUP. (COFFEE SYRUP IS MADE BY BOILING 2 TABLESPOONS OF COFFEE AND 2/3 CUP WATER TOGETHER FOR 5 MINUTES. STRAIN.)
3. ADD MELTED BUTTER.
4. BEAT VIGOROUSLY UNTIL FROSTING IS THE CONSISTENCY OF HEAVY WHIPPED CREAM.
5. SPREAD GENEROUSLY ON CAKE AND SPRINKLE WITH CHOPPED ALMONDS, PRESSING THEM INTO THE FROSTING WITH A SLIGHT PRESSURE.

BOILED ICING

2 CUPS SIFTED WHITE SUGAR
1 CUP HOT WATER
2 EGG WHITES
1 TEASPOON VANILLA

1. ADD HOT WATER TO THE SUGAR AND STIR TO DISSOLVE.
2. COVER AND BRING TO A ROLLING BOIL. STIR WELL TO BE SURE ALL THE SUGAR HAS DISSOLVED AND THAT THE SIDES OF THE PAN CONTAIN NO UNDISSOLVED SUGAR CRYSTALS. COVER AND LET BOIL FOR A FEW SECONDS.
3. UNCOVER AND BOIL UNTIL THE SUGAR REACHES A TEMPERATURE OF 236° F. OR UNTIL IT SPINS A 2 OR 3 INCH LONG THREAD WHEN THE SYRUP IS ALLOWED TO TRICKLE FROM THE TIP OF THE SPOON. (THIS IS MANAGED BY ALLOWING A SPOONFUL OF THE SYRUP TO RUN OFF THE SPOON ABOUT A FOOT ABOVE THE SURFACE OF THE COOKING SYRUP.)
4. BEAT THE EGG WHITES UNTIL STIFF. ADD A TABLESPOON OF THE HOT SYRUP TO THEM AND BEAT, ADD ANOTHER TABLESPOON OF SYRUP AND BEAT. THIS WILL PERMIT THE EGG WHITES TO RETAIN THEIR PEAK UNTIL THE SYRUP REACHES THE THREAD STAGE. THE TRICK IS TO BEGIN BEATING THE EGG WHITES JUST A MOMENT OR TWO BEFORE THE SYRUP THREADS. PRACTICE WILL TEACH YOU WHEN THE SYRUP IS NEARING THIS STAGE. YOU WILL BE ABLE TO GAGE SOMEWHAT BY THE THICKENING OF THE SUGAR AND WATER MIXTURE AS IT COOKS. THE ADDING OF THE HOT SYRUP BY THE

SPOONFULS TO RETAIN THE PEAK OF THE BEATEN EGG WHITES WILL BE HELPFUL AND ALSO ASSURE YOU OF AN ICING THAT WILL NEVER BECOME TOO HARD AS IT REMAINS ON THE CAKE.

5. NOW ADD THE HOT SYRUP TO THE EGG WHITES BY POURING INTO THE WHITES AS YOU CONTINOUSLY WHIP THEM. THIS IS BEST ACCOMPLISHED BY USING AN ELECTRIC EGG BEATER, HOWEVER, IF YOU PLAN TO DO THIS BY HAND USE THIS METHOD:

BEAT THE EGG WHITES STIFF WITH A DOVER EGG BEATER.

IN ADDING THE HOT SYRUP AND FROM HERE ON TO THE FINISH USE A WIRE WHIP, A UTENSIL SHAPED LIKE A SPOON WITH WIRE COILED AROUND TO FORM THE WHIP.

PLACE THE BOWL CONTAINING STIFFLY BEATEN EGG WHITES IN YOUR LAP.

WHIP CONTINUOUSLY WITH YOUR RIGHT HAND AND POUR THE HOT SYRUP INTO THE BEATING EGG WHITES WITH YOUR LEFT HAND.

NEVER HAVE THE HOT SYRUP POUR MORE QUICKLY THAN YOU WOULD IF DROPPED FROM THE TIP END OF A SPOON.

BEAT UNTIL THE FROSTING IS FLUFFY AND HOLDS IT-SELF IN PEAKS OR UNTIL IT HAS LOST ITS HIGH SHEEN. ADD THE VANILLA.

THIS MUST APPEAR AS A MAJOR FEAT BUT IT IS REALLY MUCH MORE SIMPLE TO PERFECT THAN YOU WOULD BE-LIEVE UPON FIRST READING. IT IS A NEVER FAIL ICING AFTER YOU GET "THE HANG" OF IT.

53.

54.

NOTES

55.

3.

COOKIES

The good old fashioned kinds and some new cookie twists await your trial in the pages ahead. Keeping the cookie jar filled can be easy and fun. Bake an assortment and accent your tray with BONBON PUFFS. These recipes will prove helpful in planning a tea or in formal reception.

ANISE DROPS

1/2 CUP SUGAR
1/3 CUP BUTTER
1 EGG
1 CUP FLOUR
1/8 TEASPOON ANISE OIL

1. CREAM SUGAR AND BUTTER.
2. ADD SIFTED FLOUR AND BEATEN EGG AND MIX WELL. ADD ANISE OIL.
3. ROLL INTO SMALL BALLS SIZE OF A LARGE MARBLE IN THE PALMS OF THE HANDS.
4. PLACE ON WELL GREASED COOKIE SHEET AND PRESS A PECAN ON TOP OF EACH COOKIE.
5. BAKE AT 375° FOR 10 MINUTES.

4 DOZEN COOKIES.

✤

58.

BONBON PUFFS

1 CUP BOILING WATER
1/4 CUP BUTTER
1 CUP SIFTED ALL PURPOSE FLOUR
4 EGGS

1. WHEN THE WATER IS AT A ROLLING BOIL ADD THE BUTTER AND STIR TO DISSOLVE.
2. ADD THE FLOUR ALL AT ONCE AND STIR VIGOROUSLY TO PREVENT THE BATTER STICKING AND BURNING TO THE PAN.
3. COOK THE MIXTURE UNTIL IT FORMS A BALL IN THE CENTER OF THE PAN. ALLOW TO COOL.
4. ADD THE EGGS ONE AT A TIME BEATING AFTER EACH ADDITION. AN ELECTRIC BEATER IS HELPFUL FOR THIS PART OF THE WORK. NOTE THAT THE MIXTURE IS COOL BUT NOT COLD, IT IS STILL QUITE WARM BUT NOT HOT ENOUGH TO COOK THE EGGS.
5. SHAPE BY USING 2 TEASPOONS AND DROPPING ABOUT ONE THIRD OF A TEASPOONFUL ONTO WELL GREASED PANS.
6. BAKE FOR 20 MINUTES AT 375° F. OR UNTIL THERE ARE NO BEADS OF MOISTURE ON THE PUFFS.
7. ALLOW THE PUFFS TO COOL AND THEN CUT IN HALF WITH A SHARP KNIFE. THE FOLLOWING FILLINGS ARE USED:

4 CUPS SIFTED CONFECTION-ERS SUGAR
1/2 CUP MELTED BUTTER
1/2 TO 3/4 CUP VERY STIFFLY WHIPPED CREAM

59.

1 SQUARE MELTED CHOCO-
LATE

1/8 TEASPOON GREEN COLOR-
ING AND 1/8 TEASPOON
MINT FLAVORING

1/8 TEASPOON RED COLORING
AND 1/8 TEASPOON OIL OF
ROSE

1/8 TEASPOON YELLOW COL-
ORING AND 1/8 TEASPOON
LEMON EXTRACT

1. MIX THE SUGAR AND BUTTER BY CREAMING TOGETHER
AS WELL AS POSSIBLE. ADD THE WHIPPED CREAM BE-
GINNING WITH 1/2 CUP AND ADDING THE OTHER 1/4
GRADUALLY IF NEEDED. BEAT WITH A WOODEN SPOON
UNTIL THE FILLINGS ARE OF THE CONSISTENCY OF BUT-
TER CREAMS—TO ACHIEVE THIS YOU MAY NEED TO ADD
ALL THE WHIPPED CREAM. HOWEVER DO NOT GET A
MIXTURE THAT WILL NOT HOLD ITS SHAPE. THE LONGER
YOU HAND BEAT THIS MIXTURE THE LIGHTER AND FLUF-
FIER THE FILLING.

2. DIVIDE THE FILLING INTO FOUR PARTS. TO EACH PART
ADD ONE OF THE FLAVORINGS AND COLORING. BEAT
WELL TO RETAIN THE WHIPPED CREAM CONSISTENCY.

3. FILL THE HALVED PUFFS WITH THE VARIOUS FILLINGS.
BY PLACING THE FILLING IN A PASTRY TUBE YOU CAN
FILL BY FORCING A ROSE DESIGN INTO THE PUFF. THE
USE OF THE TUBE FOR FILLING IS MOST DESIRABLE AL-
THOUGH YOU MAY DO SO WITH A SMALL SPOON IF
NEED BE.

4. PLACE THE FILLED PUFFS IN THE REFRIGERATOR FOR 2
HOURS.

YIELD 50 TO 60 PUFFS.

60.

CINNAMON DOUGHNUT HOLES

1 CUP SUGAR
2 EGGS, WELL BEATEN
4 TABLESPOONS MELTED
LARD
1 CUP SWEET MILK
4 TEASPOONS BAKING
POWDER
4 CUPS FLOUR
1 TEASPOON NUTMEG
1 TEASPOON SALT

1. MIX SUGAR, NUTMEG AND SALT. ADD BEATEN EGGS.
2. ADD MELTED LARD AND BEAT WELL.
3. ADD SIFTED FLOUR AND BAKING POWDER ALTERNATELY WITH THE MILK AND BEAT WELL TOGETHER.
4. TOSS ON LIGHTLY FLOURED PASTRY BOARD AND ROLL OUT 1/2 INCH THICK. CUT ROUNDS SIZE OF A DOUGH-NUT HOLE. USE THE CENTER OF A DOUGHNUT CUTTER FOR THIS PURPOSE. FRY AS YOU CUT THEM IN DEEP FAT AT 350° F. FOR ABOUT 2 OR 3 MINUTES UNTIL NICELY BROWNED.
5. TOSS THE DOUGHNUT IN CINNAMON SUGAR WHILE HOT.

CINNAMON SUGAR

1 CUP GRANULATED SUGAR
2 TEASPOONS CINNAMON

1. MIX THE TWO INGREDIENTS TOGETHER.

THIS RECIPE WILL MAKE APPROXIMATELY 36 MEDIUM DOUGHNUTS OR 200 DOUGHNUT HOLES. THE HOLES ARE PARTICULARLY ACCEPTABLE AT TEA AND ESPECIALLY IF SERVED WHILE WARM.

CINNAMON CRUNCH

USE BAKED DINNER ROLLS
USE RECIPE FOR CINNAMON
    SUGAR SUBSTITUTING
    BROWN SUGAR FOR GRAN-
    ULATED SUGAR.

1. SPLIT DINNER ROLLS.
2. SPREAD GENEROUSLY WITH BUTTER.
3. COVER TOPS WELL WITH CINNAMON BROWN SUGAR.
4. BAKE IN A 450° OVEN UNTIL CRISPY. SERVE HOT.

CHINESE ALMOND CAKES

1 CUP RICE FLOUR (CAN BE PURCHASED IN HEALTH FOOD SHOPS)

4 TABLESPOONS LARD

1 EGG

2 TABLESPOONS ALMOND OIL (SWEET ALMOND OIL MAY BE PURCHASED AT A DRUG STORE)

1 CUP SUGAR

1 TEASPOON BAKING POWDER

1½ TEASPOONS ALMOND EXTRACT

½ CUP CHOPPED FINE ALMONDS

¼ TEASPOON SALT

1. CREAM THE LARD, ADD SUGAR AND CREAM WELL.
2. ADD OIL AND CREAM WELL TOGETHER. (SESAME SEED OIL OR PEANUT OIL MAY BE SUBSTITUTED.)
3. BEAT EGG WELL AND ADD TO ABOVE. WHIP TOGETHER TO FORM A FLUFFY MIXTURE.
4. ADD ALMOND EXTRACT AND BEAT WELL.
5. ADD FLOUR, BAKING POWDER. SALT AND NUTS. BEAT WELL.
6. FORM INTO BALLS THE SIZE OF A WALNUT AND PLACE A HALF ALMOND ON THE TOP OF EACH BALL. PUT ON GREASED COOKIE SHEETS PLACING THEM ABOUT 2 INCHES APART.
7. BAKE 20 MINUTES AT 350° F.

3 DOZEN COOKIES.

63.

CHRISTMAS COOKIES 1900 or
JUST SUGAR COOKIES

1 CUP BUTTER
2 CUPS SUGAR
1/2 CUP BUTTERMILK
3 EGGS WELL BEATEN
1 1/4 TEASPOONS SODA
1/2 TEASPOON FRESHLY
 GRATED NUTMEG. (THE
 WHOLE NUTMEGS ARE
 GRATED ON A LEMON
 RIND GRATER.)
4 CUPS SIFTED FLOUR

1. CREAM BUTTER AND SUGAR.
2. ADD EGGS AND MIX WELL.
3. ADD FLOUR AND NUTMEG ALTERNATELY WITH THE BUT-
   TERMILK AND SODA (WHICH ARE MIXED TOGETHER).
4. MIX ALL INGREDIENTS WELL.
5. CHILL AND ROLL TO JUST LESS THAN 1/4 INCH THICK.
6. CUT IN ROUND SHAPES AND SPRINKLE WITH SUGAR.
7. PLACE ON A WELL GREASED COOKIE SHEET AND BAKE
   AT 375° F. FOR 8 TO 10 MINUTES.

YIELD: 150 COOKIES.

64.

FOR CHRISTMAS COOKIES USE THE FOLLOWING METHOD:

ROLL THE COOKIES AND CUT IN FANCY SHAPES OR ANIMAL AND OTHER DESIGNS. DO NOT SPRINKLE WITH SUGAR BEFORE BAKING. AFTER THE COOKIE IS BAKED AND HAS COOLED FROST WITH THE FOLLOWING ICING:

> 3 CUPS SIFTED CONFEC-
> TIONERS SUGAR
> 1/4 CUP MELTED BUTTER
> 4 TABLESPOONS CREAM

1. ADD BUTTER TO THE SUGAR AND CREAM TOGETHER. ADD CREAM AND BEAT WELL TO FORM A SMOOTH FROSTING.
2. ICE THE COOKIE AND DECORATE WITH VARIOUS COLORED SUGARS, SILVER DRAGEES AND CINNAMON IMPERIALS. YOUR OWN IMAGINATION WILL DIRECT YOUR DECORATIONS.

HE WHO AS A CHILD HAS MISSED THE GLORIOUS FESTIVITIES OF BAKING AND DECORATING THE CHRISTMAS COOKIES HAS INDEED MISSED ONE OF THE SIMPLE CHILDHOOD PLEAURES OF THE YULETIDE SEASON.

COCONUT AND ROLLED OAT COOKIES

1 CUP BUTTER
2 CUPS BROWN SUGAR
(FIRMLY PACKED)
2 EGGS
2 CUPS FLOUR
2 TEASPOONS SODA
1 TEASPOON BAKING
POWDER
1 TEASPOON SALT
1 TEASPOON VANILLA
2 CUPS QUICK OATS
2 CUPS COCONUT

1. CREAM SUGAR AND SHORTENING.
2. ADD EGGS AND MIX WELL. ADD COCONUT, OATS AND MIX.
3. ADD SIFTED FLOUR, SODA, BAKING POWDER, SALT AND VANILLA. MIX WELL. THIS MAKES A VERY STIFF BATTER. PLACE IN ICE BOX TO CHILL.
4. SHAPE IN BALLS THE SIZE OF A HICKORY NUT AND BAKE AT 325° F. FOR 12 MINUTES. WILL MAKE APPROXIMATELY 75 COOKIES.

CRINOLINE GINGERBREAD LEMON GLACE

½ CUP SUGAR
½ CUP BUTTER
1 CUP MOLASSES
1 CUP BOILING WATER
WITH 2 LEVEL TEASPOONS
BAKING SODA
2½ CUPS FLOUR
1 TEASPOON EACH OF
CLOVES, CINNAMON AND
GINGER
2 WELL BEATEN EGGS

1. CREAM BUTTER AND SUGAR.
2. STIR MOLASSES IN WELL.
3. SIFT FLOUR WITH SPICES AND ADD ALTERNATELY WITH
   THE BOILING WATER, BEGINNING AND ENDING WITH
   THE FLOUR. IN MIXING SODA AND BOILING WATER,
   POUR BOILING WATER ON THE SODA AND MIX.
4. BEAT IN EGGS WELL.
5. THIS IS A VERY THIN BATTER. BAKE IN GREASED 9x12
   INCH PAN AT 350° F. FOR 30 MINUTES.
6. COOL AND FROST WITH LEMON GLACE.

MIX TOGETHER ½ CUP SIFTED CONFECTIONERS SUGAR
WITH 1 TABLESPOON AND 2 TEASPOONS OF MILK. BEAT
WELL TOGETHER AND ADD ½ TEASPOON OF LEMON
EXTRACT.

SPREAD THE GLACE OVER THE CAKE AND ALLOW TO SET.

DATE BARS

¾ CUP BROWN SUGAR
½ CUP BUTTER
¾ CUP FLOUR

1. CREAM BUTTER AND SUGAR, THEN WORK IN THE FLOUR. PAT THIS IN A SHALLOW TIN, 8x12 INCH PAN, WARM THE PAN BEFORE PUTTING THE MIXTURE IN AND IT WILL SPREAD EASIER.
2. BAKE 10 MINUTES AT 350° F.

1¼ CUPS BROWN SUGAR
2 EGGS
¼ TEASPOON SALT
1 TEASPOON VANILLA
2½ TABLESPOONS OF FLOUR SIFTED WITH ¾ TEASPOON BAKING POWDER
½ CUP COCONUT
1 CUP PECANS
½ CUP OF CUT DATES (USE SCISSORS TO CUT DATES)

1. WHILE THE FIRST MIXTURE IS BAKING YOU CAN MIX THE BROWN SUGAR WITH THE EGGS, ADD THE SIFTED FLOUR AND BAKING POWDER. THEN ALL OTHER INGREDIENTS.
2. SPREAD THIS OVER THE FIRST MIXTURE WHEN YOU TAKE IT FROM THE OVEN.
3. BAKE ALL THIS 20 MINUTES AT 350° F.
4. CUT IN SMALL SQUARES WHEN COOL.

54 DATE BARS.

68.

DATE CONFECTIONS

1 CUP DATES (USE SCISSORS
TO CUT). FIRST CUT
LENGTHWISE AND THEN
CUT INTO SMALL BITS.
1 LEVEL TEASPOON SODA
1 CUP SUGAR
1 CUP BOILING WATER
2 TABLESPOONS BUTTER
1 EGG
1 1/3 CUPS SIFTED FLOUR
½ CUP NUTS (CUT)

1. POUR BOILING WATER MIXED WITH SODA OVER CUT
   DATES.
2. CREAM BUTTER AND SUGAR, ADD BEATEN EGG YOLK.
3. ADD DATES AND FLOUR (TO WHICH NUTS HAVE BEEN
   MIXED TO SEPARATE NUT PARTICLES).
4. BEAT WELL AND FOLD IN STIFFLY BEATEN EGG WHITE.
5. BAKE IN A 9x12 INCH PAN AT 325° F. FOR 40 MINUTES.
6. ALLOW TO COOL, CUT IN SMALL SQUARES AND SIFT
   POWDERED SUGAR OVER THE PIECES. USE GENEROUS
   AMOUNT OF CONFECTIONERS SUGAR.

DATE FILLED COOKIES

2½ CUPS FLOUR
1 CUP BROWN SUGAR
1 CUP BUTTER
1 TEASPOON SODA
2½ CUPS ROLLED OATS
½ CUP HOT WATER
½ TEASPOON SALT

1. SIFT FLOUR AND MEASURE.
2. CREAM SUGAR AND BUTTER, MEASURE BROWN SUGAR BY PACKING TIGHTLY INTO THE CUP FOR FULL MEASUREMENT.
3. ADD FLOUR, OATS AND SALT TOGETHER WITH THE SODA ADDED TO THE HOT WATER.
4. MIX WELL. PLACE ON FLOURED BOARD AND ROLL TO JUST A LITTLE LESS THAN ¼ INCH THICK. CUT IN ROUNDS. BAKE ON WELL GREASED COOKIE SHEET AT 375° F. FOR 12 MINUTES. REMOVE FROM PAN WHEN COOLED AND PUT TOGETHER WITH THE FOLLOWING FILLING:

1 LB. DATES
1 CUP SUGAR
½ CUP WATER

1. CUT DATES WITH SCISSORS INTO SMALL PIECES BY FIRST CUTTING THE DATES LENGTHWISE, THEN INTO SMALL PIECES.
2. ADD SUGAR, THEN WATER. COOK SLOWLY TO THICKEN. COOL.
3. FILL COOKIES BY SPREADING A TEASPOON OF THIS MIXTURE ON THE FLAT SIDE OF A COOKIE, THEN PLACE FLAT SIDE OF ANOTHER COOKIE ON TOP OF THE FILLING.

70.

DATE SQUARES

1 CUP SUGAR
5 EGGS BEATEN SEPARATELY
1½ TEASPOONS OF BAKING
POWDER
1 CUP FLOUR
1 CUP CHOPPED DATES
1 CUP CHOPPED WALNUTS
¼ TEASPOON SALT

1. CREAM SUGAR WITH BEATEN EGG YOLKS.
2. SIFT AND MEASURE FLOUR. ADD THE BAKING POWDER
   SALT, DATES AND NUTS TOSSING ALL TOGETHER.
3. ADD FLOUR TO FIRST MIXTURE. MIX WELL.
4. ADD STIFFLY BEATEN EGG WHITES BY FOLDING INTO
   MIXTURE LAST.
5. BAKE IN A GREASED PAN 10x14 INCHES FOR 20 TO 25
   MINUTES AT 350° F.
6. CUT IN SQUARES, COOL AND SIFT A GENEROUS AMOUNT
   OF CONFECTIONERS SUGAR OVER THE CAKES.

32 SQUARES, 1½ INCH EACH.

✢

1 DOZEN COOKIES

1 CUP (PACKED) BROWN
SUGAR
2 EGG WHITES
1/4 CUP OF CUT RAISINS
1/4 CUP CUT DATES
1/4 CUP CHOPPED PECANS
1/2 CUP SHREDDED COCO-
NUT (UNSWEETENED)
1 TEASPOON VANILLA

1. SIFT BROWN SUGAR AND ADD TO THE STIFFLY BEATEN
EGG WHITES.
2. STIR IN THE OTHER INGREDIENTS. ADD VANILLA.
3. DROP FROM A SPOON ONTO A VERY WELL GREASED
COOKIE SHEET.
4. BAKE AT 350° F. FOR 20 MINUTES. ALLOW TO COOL AND
TAKE FROM PAN BY RUNNING A SPATULA UNDER EACH
COOKIE. THEY ARE DIFFICULT TO REMOVE IN SHAPE BUT
IT CAN BE DONE WITH PATIENCE AND IS WELL WORTH
THE TROUBLE.

SIZE OF COOKIE DETERMINES THE NUMBER. THE RECIPE
MAKES 1 DOZEN LARGE COOKIES.

FAYES

6 OUNCES BUTTER
3½ OUNCES BAKING CHOCOLATE
4 EGGS
2 CUPS SUGAR
½ TEASPOON SALT
1 TEASPOON VANILLA
1 CUP FLOUR, SIFT BEFORE MEASURING
1 CUP BROKEN PECANS, COARSELY

1. MELT THE CHOCOLATE AND BUTTER IN TOP OF DOUBLE BOILER. COOL.
2. BEAT THE EGGS LIGHTLY.
3. ADD THE SUGAR TO THE EGGS. MIX TOGETHER. ADD THE SALT AND VANILLA.
4. BEAT TOGETHER LIGHTLY. ADD THE CHOCOLATE AND BUTTER MIXTURE.
5. MIX THE PECANS WITH THE SIFTED FLOUR AND ADD TO THE LIQUID MIXTURE. FOLD TOGETHER ONLY ENOUGH TO MIX WELL.
6. BAKE IN A LIGHTLY GREASED 8 X 11 INCH PAN AT 325° F FOR FIFTY MINUTES.
7. CUT IN SQUARES WHILE WARM.

FAYES HAVE A CRUNCHY LIKE TOP AND BOTTOM CRUST WITH AN ALMOST CHOCOLATE CREAM CENTER. YOU WILL WISH YOU HAD DOUBLED THE BATCH FOR THIS IS THE "NOTHING THAN WHICHER."

FRUIT MUSHROOMS

1½ CUPS BROWN SUGAR
(FIRMLY PACKED)
1 CUP SHORTENING
3 EGGS
1 CUP COCONUT
1 CUP PECANS
1 CUP DATES (CUT FINE,
USING SCISSORS)
1¾ CUPS FLOUR
1¼ CUPS OATMEAL (PLACE
OATMEAL IN AN ONION
CHOPPER, A GLASS CUP IN
WHICH THE TOP FITS
DOWN WITH A CHOPPER
ATTACHED TO MINCE THE
ONION. THIS WILL FINELY
MINCE THE O A T M E A L
WHICH IS NECESSARY.)
1 TEASPOON SODA DIS-
SOLVED IN 2 T A B L E -
SPOONS HOT WATER
½ TEASPOON SALT
½ TEASPOON CINNAMON
1 TEASPOON VANILLA

1. CREAM SUGAR AND SHORTENING.
2. ADD BEATEN EGGS AND MIX WELL UNTIL FLUFFY.
3. SIFT FLOUR AND ADD OATMEAL, THEN DATES, COCONUT,
   NUTS, FLAVORINGS AND SODA. MIX ALL THESE ITEMS
   INTO THE FLUFFY MIXTURE.
4. DROP BY TEASPOONFULS ONTO A WELL GREASED
   COOKIE SHEET AND BAKE FOR 15 MINUTES AT 350° F.

74.

PECAN SIGHS

1/4 LB. BUTTER
1/4 LB. CONFECTIONERS
SUGAR
1 CUP AND 2 TABLESPOONS
WHOLE WHEAT FLOUR
3/4 CUP CHOPPED NUTS
1/2 TEASPOON VANILLA
ADDITIONAL CONFECTIONERS
SUGAR MAY BE USED FOR ROLL-
ING THE BAKED COOKIE.

1. CREAM BUTTER AND SUGAR.
2. WORK IN, BY RUBBING WITH THE HANDS, THE SIFTED
   FLOUR, NUTS AND VANILLA.
3. SHAPE INTO BALLS THE SIZE OF A HICKORY NUT. PLACE
   ON A WELL GREASED COOKIE SHEET AND BAKE AT 300° F.
   FOR 20 TO 25 MINUTES.
4. REMOVE FROM THE PAN TO THE CONFECTIONERS SUGAR
   AND COAT THEM WELL ALL OVER.

THIS RECIPE MAKES APPROXIMATELY 35 SIGHS.

SANTA CLAUS CAKES

3 WHOLE EGGS
I TEASPOON VANILLA
¾ CUP FLOUR
I TEASPOON BAKING POWDER
I CUP SUGAR
I CUP WALNUTS
I LB. CUT DATES (USE SCISSORS TO CUT)

1. BEAT EGGS LIGHTLY. ADD VANILLA.
2. SIFT FLOUR, BAKING POWDER AND SUGAR TOGETHER. MIX WELL WITH DATES AND NUTS.
3. MIX EGGS WITH DRY INGREDIENTS.
4. SPREAD ABOUT ½ INCH THICK ON A WELL GREASED BAKING SHEET.
5. BAKE AT 350° F. FOR 35 MINUTES.
6. CUT WHILE WARM INTO SMALL BARS AND ROLL IN GRANULATED SUGAR.

THIS RECIPE MAKES 48 SMALL BARS. WHILE THE NAME IMPLIES A CHRISTMAS COOKIE IT IS A FAVORITE AND YOU WILL FIND WILLING CONSUMERS AT ANY SEASON OF THE YEAR.

76.

SOFT GINGER COOKIES

¾ CUP BUTTERMILK
¾ TABLESPOON VINEGAR
1¼ CUPS SHORTENING
1¼ CUPS SUGAR
1 EGG
¼ CUP MOLASSES
3¼ CUPS SIFTED FLOUR
2 TEASPOONS BAKING SODA
1 TEASPOON GINGER
1 TEASPOON CINNAMON
1 TEASPOON SALT

1. CREAM SHORTENING AND SUGAR.
2. ADD BEATEN EGG AND MIX WELL.
3. ADD MOLASSES AND VINEGAR. MIX WELL.
4. SIFT THE FLOUR, BAKING SODA, SPICES AND SALT.
5. ADD MILK ALTERNATING WITH THE FLOUR, BEGINNING AND ENDING WITH SOME OF THE FLOUR. MIX WELL.
6. DROP BY TEASPOONFULS ONTO A WELL GREASED COOKIE SHEET.
7. BAKE AT 375° F. TO 400° F. FOR 12 MINUTES.

85 COOKIES.

SOUR CREAM DROP COOKIES

2¼ CUPS BROWN SUGAR
¾ CUP SHORTENING
2 EGGS
1 CUP SOUR CREAM
¾ TEASPOON SALT
¼ TEASPOON NUTMEG
1 TEASPOON SODA
4 TEASPOONS BAKING POWDER
4½ CUPS SIFTED FLOUR
1 CUP RAISINS
1 CUP NUTS

1. CREAM SHORTENING AND SUGAR.
2. ADD EGGS AND BEAT WELL.
3. SIFT FLOUR, SPICES AND BAKING POWDER. MIX SODA WITH SOUR CREAM. ALTERNATE FLOUR MIXTURE WITH CREAM BEGINNING AND ENDING WITH SOME OF THE FLOUR. ADD CHOPPED NUTS AND RAISINS. MIX WELL.
4. DROP BY TEASPOONFULS ONTO A WELL GREASED COOKIE SHEET.
5. BAKE AT 400° F. FOR 12 MINUTES.

YIELD 130 SMALL COOKIES.

NOTES

79.

80.

NOTES

81.

4.

DESSERTS AND PUDDINGS

If you are in search of a dessert "fit for a king" make THREE WAYS TO HEAVEN. As a suggestion, TROPICAL, WHAT IS IT? or ANGEL FOOD ROYAL are "quickies" and certain to please.

ANGEL FOOD ROYALE

1 CUP ROYAL ANNE CHERRY JUICE
1/4 CUP CORNSTARCH
4 EGG YOLKS
1 CUP ROYAL ANNE CHERRIES, CUT IN HALF
1/4 CUP MARASCHINO CHERRIES, CUT IN HALF
1/2 CUP CHOPPED NUTS
1 CUP PINEAPPLE JUICE
1/2 CUP SUGAR
1 CUP PINEAPPLE TIDBITS
2 CUPS WHIPPED CREAM
1 ANGEL FOOD CAKE

1. MIX THE CORNSTARCH WITH THE COLD FRUIT JUICES. COOK IN A DOUBLE BOILER UNTIL THICKENED.
2. ADD THE BEATEN EGG YOLKS AND COOK 5 MINUTES.
3. COOL AND ADD THE STIFFLY WHIPPED CREAM AND FOLD IN THE FRUITS.
4. SERVE OVER SLICES OF ANGEL FOOD CAKE.

THIS WILL SERVE TWELVE PEOPLE.

84.

CLEAR BUTTERSCOTCH SAUCE

2 CUPS BROWN SUGAR
¾ CUPS WATER
1½ TEASPOON CORNSTARCH
2 TABLESPOONS BUTTER

1. MIX SUGAR AND WATER. BOIL FOR 10 MINUTES ON MEDIUM HEAT.
2. DISSOLVE THE CORNSTARCH IN ¼ CUP COLD WATER AND ADD TO HOT MIXTURE. STIR WELL TO MIX.
3. BOIL 5 MINUTES.
4. REMOVE FROM THE FIRE AND ADD THE BUTTER. STIR.
5. ALLOW SAUCE TO COOL OR IF DESIRED YOU MAY SERVE WARM.

THIS SAUCE MAY BE USED FOR BOTH PUDDINGS OR ICE CREAM TOPPING.

ECLAIR OF FRESH FRUITS WITH WHIPPED CREAM

6 ECLAIR SHELLS
4 SLICED BANANAS
2 ORANGES
1/2 FRESH PINEAPPLE
3 PEACHES
1 PINT WHIPPED CREAM
1/2 CUP CONFECTIONERS
SUGAR
1 CUP CHOPPED NUTS

1. PREPARE THE ECLAIR SHELLS BY USING THE RECIPE FOR BONBON PUFFS AND SHAPING THE SHELL WITH A SPOONFUL POURED ALONG THE EDGE OF A KNIFE IN ORDER TO OBTAIN A FINGER LIKE SHAPE. WHEN SHELL IS BAKED AND COOLED FILL WITH THE FRUIT MIXTURE.
2. CUT ALL THE FRUITS INTO SMALL PIECES AND MIX TO-GETHER WITH VERY STIFFLY WHIPPED CREAM AND 1/2 CUP OF CONFECTIONERS SUGAR.
3. PILE THE FILLING INTO THE SHELL AND SERVE WITH A DASH OF WHIPPED CREAM ON THE TOP AND A SPRIN-KLING OF CHOPPED NUTS.

THIS DESSERT IS SIMPLE YET SPECIAL FOR THAT PARTICULAR PARTY. THE ECLAIR SHELLS MIGHT BE PURCHASED AT THE BAKERY, UNFILLED OF COURSE, AND BE A HELPFUL HINT FOR THOSE LAST MINUTE INVITED GUESTS.

FLEUR d'ORANGE

4 EGG YOLKS
I CUP SUGAR
JUICE AND GRATED RIND
OF I ORANGE
I TABLESPOON LEMON
JUICE
I PINT WHIPPED CREAM
ANGEL FOOD CAKE
I QUART ICE CREAM
I CUP CHOPPED PECANS
2 TEASPOONS NUTMEG
(FRESHLY GRATED)

1. BEAT EGG YOLKS WELL, ADD SUGAR AND CONTINUE BEATING.
2. ADD LEMON AND ORANGE JUICE.
3. PLACE ON FIRE IN A DOUBLE BOILER. STIR FREQUENTLY AND ALLOW TO COOK UNTIL THE EGG MIXTURE COOKS DOWN AND THICKENS. ADD ORANGE RIND. COOL.
4. FOLD IN WHIPPED CREAM.
5. CUT ANGEL CAKE AS FOR SERVING AND PLACE A MOUND OF VANILLA ICE CREAM ON TOP OF THE CAKE. OVER THIS SERVE THE ORANGE SAUCE.
6. SPRINKLE TOP WITH A BIT OF GRATED NUTMEG AND CHOPPED PECANS.

THIS WILL SERVE 8 TO 10 GUESTS.

FROZEN CHOCOLATE CRUNCH

1 CUP CHOPPED PECANS
3 CUPS CHOCOLATE CAKE
CRUMBS. (THESE MAY BE
MADE BY CRUMBLING
CHOCOLATE CAKE INTO
FINE SMOOTH CRUMBS.)
1 QT. VANILLA ICE CREAM,
FRENCH VANILLA
PREFERRED.

1. MIX THE CHOPPED NUTS WITH THE CAKE CRUMBS.
2. ROLL THE ICE CREAM WHICH HAS BEEN SHAPED INTO
   BALLS USING AN ICE CREAM DISHER OR A TEA CUP INTO
   CRUMB MIXTURE.
3. PLACE IN THE FREEZING COMPARTMENT OF YOUR RE-
   FRIGERATOR AND ALLOW TO FREEZE.
4. BEFORE SERVING TIME IT IS BEST TO PERMIT THE CRUNCH
   TO PRE-THAW SOMEWHAT IN ORDER TO REMOVE THE
   ROCK LIKE TEXTURE HARD FROZEN CREAM CAN HAVE.
5. SERVE WITH A GENEROUS AMOUNT OF WHIPPED CREAM,
   SWEETENED AND FLAVORED WITH VANILLA.

THIS WILL MAKE 8 SERVINGS, UNLESS YOU LIKE LARGE
SERVINGS THEN THE SIZE OF ICE CREAM BALL WILL DETER-
MINE THE NUMBER OF GUESTS YOU MAY SERVE.

FROZEN TOASTED ALMOND BALL WITH HOT FUDGE

2 CUPS CHOPPED TOASTED
ALMONDS
2 CUPS HOT FUDGE SAUCE
1 QUART OF FRENCH
VANILLA ICE CREAM

1. SHAPE THE ICE CREAM INTO BALLS USING AN ICE CREAM DISHER OR A TEA CUP AND SPOON.
2. ROLL THE ICE CREAM IN THE CHOPPED ALMONDS TO COAT WELL.
3. PLACE IN SHERBET GLASSES AND SERVE WITH A GENEROUS AMOUNT OF HOT FUDGE SAUCE.

⁜

HOT FUDGE SAUCE

1 CUP COCOA
2 CUPS BROWN SUGAR
1 CUP WHITE SUGAR
1/8 TEASPOON SALT
2 CUPS WATER
3 TABLESPOONS BUTTER
1 TEASPOON VANILLA
2 TABLESPOONS
  CORNSTARCH

1. SIFT THE SUGAR, COCOA, SALT AND CORNSTARCH.
2. ADD THE WATER AND MIX. PLACE OVER DIRECT FIRE TO COOK.
3. STIR UNTIL WELL MIXED AND MIXTURE BEGINS TO BOIL.
4. REDUCE HEAT TO LOW AND COOK UNTIL MIXTURE REACHES 200° F. OR UNTIL IT THICKENS TO THE CONSISTENCY OF THICK CREAM.
5. REMOVE FROM FIRE AND ADD THE BUTTER AND VANILLA.
6. ALLOW TO COOL SOMEWHAT BEFORE SERVING.

THIS SAUCE MAY BE USED AS A PUDDING SAUCE AS WELL AS AN ICE CREAM SAUCE OR FOR CHOCOLATE MILK MIXTURES.

LEMON FLUFF TORTE

12 EGG WHITES
3 CUPS SUGAR
1 TEASPOON VANILLA

1. BEAT EGG WHITES UNTIL VERY DRY.
2. ADD SUGAR GRADUALLY, BEATING CONSTANTLY.
3. ADD VANILLA. BEAT 15 MINUTES. THIS IS WHERE AN ELECTRIC BEATER IS USEFUL.
4. SPREAD ON BROWN WRAPPING PAPER WHICH HAS BEEN BUTTERED ON BOTH SIDES. PLACE ON A COOKIE SHEET.
5. BAKE AT 300° F. FOR 1½ HOURS.
6. WHEN COOL CUT IN SQUARES AND SERVE WITH THIS TOPPING:

6 EGG YOLKS
1½ CUPS ORANGE JUICE
RIND AND JUICE OF 1 LEMON
GRATED RIND OF 3 ORANGES
1 CUP SUGAR
1 TEASPOON BUTTER
2 TABLESPOONS FLOUR

1. MIX BEATEN EGG YOLKS WITH THE OTHER INGREDIENTS.
2. COOK IN A DOUBLE BOILER 15 MINUTES. STIR FREQUENTLY. COOL.
3. AS YOU SERVE EACH SQUARE TOP WITH WHIPPED CREAM AND SPRINKLE WITH TOASTED ALMONDS.

THIS IS A DELECTABLE AND RATHER EXTRAVAGANT LOOKING DESSERT.

MINCE MEAT UPSIDE DOWN CAKE

1½ CUPS SUGAR
¾ CUP BUTTER
3½ CUPS FLOUR
1½ CUPS MILK
3½ TEASPOONS BAKING
POWDER
3 EGGS

1. CREAM BUTTER AND SUGAR, BEAT IN EGGS.
2. ADD MILK AND FLOUR (WHICH HAS BEEN SIFTED WITH BAKING POWDER) ALTERNATELY.

SPREAD FOR BOTTOM PAN

1½ CUPS MINCE MEAT
1½ CUPS CHOPPED APPLES
¼ CUP ORANGE JUICE
½ CUP SUGAR
2 TABLESPOONS MELTED
BUTTER
½ CUP BROWN SUGAR

1. IN BOTTOM OF PAN PUT MELTED BUTTER AND BROWN SUGAR.
2. OVER THIS PLACE MINCE MEAT MIXTURE.
3. POUR CAKE BATTER OVER ALL. BAKE IN OVEN 375° F. FOR 40 MINUTES.
4. TURN UPSIDE DOWN. CUT IN SQUARES AND SERVE WITH WHIPPED CREAM.

MONT BLANC

1½ CUPS MILK
¾ CUP BROWN SUGAR
¾ CUP GRANULATED SUGAR
3 CUPS WHIPPED CREAM
1 CUP CHOPPED TOASTED
   CHESTNUTS (TOASTED
   SHAVED ALMONDS MAY
   BE SUBSTITUTED)
1 QT. FRENCH VANILLA ICE
   CREAM

1. BOIL THE SUGARS AND MILK UNTIL IT FORMS A SOFT BALL IN COLD WATER. COOL AND ADD 2 CUPS WHIPPED CREAM.
2. SERVE BY PLACING 2 TABLESPOONS OF THE SAUCE IN BOTTOM OF A STEMMED SHERBET, SPRINKLE A FEW OF THE NUTS ON THIS, THEN PLACE A SERVING OF ICE CREAM ON TOP OF THIS (A ROUND SCOOP IS PREFERRED). NEXT, ADD MORE OF THE CUSTARD AROUND THE SIDES OF THE ICE CREAM AND SPRINKLE WITH THE NUTS. TOP THE ICE CREAM WITH PLAIN WHIPPED CREAM. SERVE A PLAIN SALTINE WITH THIS DESSERT.

THIS WILL SERVE 6 OR 8 GUESTS.

93.

NUT TORTE

1/2 CUP SUGAR
1/2 CUP BUTTER
4 EGG YOLKS
5 TABLESPOONS MILK
I CUP AND I TABLESPOON
FLOUR, SIFT BEFORE
MEASURING
1 1/2 TEASPOONS BAKING
POWDER
5 EGG WHITES
3/4 CUP CHOPPED NUTS
I CUP SUGAR
I TEASPOON VANILLA

1. CREAM BUTTER AND SUGAR.
2. ADD BEATEN EGG YOLKS.
3. SIFT FLOUR AND BAKING POWDER, THEN ADD WITH THE MILK.
4. PUT BATTER IN TWO LAYER TINS WELL OILED.
5. BEAT EGG WHITES TO A STIFF FROTH AND ADD THE SUGAR BEATING AS YOU MAKE THIS ADDITION. FOLD IN THE VANILLA. SPREAD OVER BATTER. SPRINKLE WITH NUTS. BAKE 30 MINUTES AT 300° F.
6. PREPARE THE FOLLOWING FILLING:

FILLING

1 CUP MILK
¾ CUP SUGAR
1 TABLESPOON CORN-
STARCH
1 EGG YOLK
1 TABLESPOON BUTTER
1 TEASPOON VANILLA

1. BEAT EGG YOLK AND ADD SUGAR.
2. BLEND CORNSTARCH WITH THE MILK AND ADD TO THE
EGG MIXTURE. ADD THE VANILLA.
3. COOK IN A DOUBLE BOILER UNTIL THICKENED. ADD
BUTTER.
4. SPREAD BETWEEN THE TWO TORTE LAYERS.
SERVE WITH A GENEROUS AMOUNT OF WHIPPED CREAM.

✤

PEACH LUSCIOUS

1/2 CUP SUGAR
2 EGGS, SEPARATED
4 TABLESPOONS VEGETABLE SHORTENING
GRATED RIND OF 1 LEMON
1 TABLESPOON LEMON JUICE
2/3 CUP MILK
1 1/4 CUPS FLOUR
3 TEASPOONS BAKING POWDER
1/2 TEASPOON SALT
8 TO 10 LARGE FRESH PEACHES
2/3 CUP SUGAR
1/4 CUP CONFECTIONERS SUGAR

1. BEAT EGG YOLKS, ADD THE SUGAR. SOFTEN SHORTENING TO ROOM TEMPERATURE. BLEND TOGETHER.
2. ADD THE SIFTED DRY INGREDIENTS AND LEMON RIND ALTERNATELY WITH THE MILK.
3. RUB THE SIDES OF A WIDE SHALLOW BAKING DISH WITH BUTTER.
4. FILL THE BOTTOM OF THE DISH WITH THE PEELED AND SLICED PEACHES. SPRINKLE THE 2/3 CUP SUGAR AND LEMON JUICE OVER THE PEACHES.
5. POUR THE BATTER OVER THE TOP. BAKE AT 350° F. FOR 45 MINUTES.
6. REMOVE FROM THE OVEN AND COVER WITH A MERINGUE MADE BY BEATING THE EGG WHITES UNTIL STIFF AND FOLDING IN THE CONFECTIONERS SUGAR.
7. BROWN THE MERINGUE AT 325° F. FOR 15 MINUTES.
8. SERVE WARM WITH WHIPPED OR THICK CREAM.

THIS TASTY PUDDING MAY ALSO BE MADE BY USING CANNED PEACHES. BE SURE TO POUR THE JUICE FROM THE CAN OVER PEACHES BEFORE ADDING THE SUGAR IN STEP NUMBER FOUR.

96.

PINEAPPLE MACHE

1 PACKAGE LEMON GELA-
TINE DESSERT
2 CUPS DRAINED, CRUSHED,
CANNED PINEAPPLE
1 PINT WHIPPING CREAM
1 CUP SUGAR
12 MARASCHINO CHERRIES

1. PREPARE LEMON GELATINE AS DIRECTED ON PACKAGE.
2. WHEN COOL ADD THE PINEAPPLE AND SUGAR.
3. AS THE GELATINE BEGINS TO THICKEN CONSIDERABLY
   FOLD IN THE WHIPPED CREAM.
4. FILL 12 SHERBET CUPS AND PLACE A CHERRY ON TOP.
5. SERVE WITH PLAIN CAKE OR COOKIES.

THIS IS A LIGHT AND PLEASANT DESSERT.

✤

ROYAL CHOCOLATE, GOLDEN LION

4 EGG YOLKS, WELL BEATEN
1/2 POUND BUTTER
1 CUP POWDERED SUGAR
1/2 POUND BAKING
    CHOCOLATE
1 TEASPOON VANILLA
4 EGG WHITES STIFFLY
    BEATEN

1. CREAM THE BUTTER AND SUGAR.
2. MELT THE CHOCOLATE IN THE TOP OF A DOUBLE BOILER.
3. ADD THE EGG YOLKS TO THE CREAMED MIXTURE AND STIR WELL.
4. ADD THE CHOCOLATE. BEAT TOGETHER WELL.
5. FOLD IN THE STIFFLY BEATEN EGG WHITES.
6. SPREAD IN A BUTTERED 8 X 11 INCH PAN. REFRIGERATE FOR SEVERAL HOURS BEFORE SERVING.
7. TO SERVE: FILL SHERBET DISHES 2/3 FULL OF WARM SOFT CUSTARD AND PLACE A 1 1/2 INCH SQUARE OF THE CHOCOLATE IN THE CENTER OF THE CUSTARD.

SOFT CUSTARD

3 CUPS MILK
3 EGG YOLKS
1/8 TEASPOON SALT
1 TABLESPOON
 CORNSTARCH
1/2 CUP SUGAR
1 TEASPOON VANILLA

A. BEAT THE EGG YOLKS SLIGHTLY.

B. SIFT THE SALT, SUGAR, AND CORNSTARCH. ADD TO THE
   EGGS. MIX WELL.

C. ADD THE MILK AND BEAT ALL TOGETHER WITH THE EGG
   BEATER.

D. PLACE IN TOP OF A DOUBLE BOILER AND COOK UNTIL
   THE MIXTURE COATS A WOODEN SPOON.

E. REMOVE FROM THE FIRE AND BEAT WITH AN EGG BEATER.
   THEN COVER AND ALLOW CUSTARD TO COOL UNTIL
   WARM.

THIS IS THE ULTIMATE IN CHOCOLATE DESSERTS. I SUGGEST
THAT YOU MAKE THE CHOCOLATE PART EARLY AND ALLOW
TO REFRIGERATE. JUST BEFORE SERVING TIME MAKE THE
CUSTARD AND WHILE YOU ARE DINING THE HOT CUSTARD
WILL COOL JUST TO THE CORRECT TEMPERATURE FOR SERV-
ING AT DESSERT TIME.

SAILOR DUFF

1 CUP BROWN SUGAR
1 EGG
1/4 CUP BUTTER (DO NOT MELT)
1/4 TEASPOON VANILLA
1/4 TEASPOON SALT
1 CUP SOUR MILK AND 1 TEASPOON BAKING SODA
1 1/4 CUPS SIFTED FLOUR
1/4 TEASPOON BAKING POWDER
1/4 CUP RAISINS
1/4 CUP NUTS

1. CREAM BUTTER AND SUGAR, ADD SALT AND VANILLA.
2. ADD BEATEN EGG.
3. ADD THE FLOUR SIFTED WITH BAKING POWDER ALTERNATELY WITH MILK AND SODA. BE SURE TO BEGIN AND END WITH FLOUR.
4. STIR IN THE NUTS AND RAISINS WHICH HAVE BEEN CUT. SUGGEST USING SCISSORS TO CUT RAISINS IN PIECES.
5. FILL WELL GREASED STEAMER MOLDS OR CANS HALF FULL OF THE MIXTURE. STEAM 1 1/2 HOURS. SERVE WITH THE FOLLOWING SAUCE:
   1 PINT WHIPPED CREAM MIXED WITH 1 WHOLE BEATEN EGG.
   1/2 CUP SUGAR AND 1 TEASPOON VANILLA.

100.

THREE WAYS TO HEAVEN

6 EGGS
1 CUP SUGAR
1/4 CUP WATER
1/2 TEASPOON VANILLA
1/2 TEASPOON LEMON
   EXTRACT
1 CUP FLOUR
1/4 TEASPOON CREAM OF
   TARTAR
1/4 TEASPOON SALT

1. BEAT EGG YOLKS WELL, ADD SUGAR GRADUALLY, BEAT-
   ING WELL AFTER EACH ADDITION.
2. FOLD IN THE WATER AND FLAVORING.
3. SIFT FLOUR BEFORE MEASURING AND FOLD WELL INTO
   THE EGG MIXTURE.
4. BEAT THE EGG WHITES UNTIL FROTHY, ADD THE CREAM
   OF TARTAR AND SALT. BEAT WHITES UNTIL STIFF.
5. FOLD CAREFULLY INTO THE EGG YOLK AND FLOUR MIX-
   TURE. POUR INTO UNGREASED ANGEL FOOD PAN
   (LARGE SIZE PAN) AND BAKE 1 HOUR AT 325° F.
6. PLACE TO COOL BY INVERTING CAKE ON A RACK.
   WHEN COLD REMOVE FROM PAN BY RUNNING A KNIFE
   AROUND THE SIDES AND ALSO THE CENTER STEM.
7. SPLIT CAKE INTO THREE LAYERS WITH A SHARP KNIFE.
8. FILL WITH THE FOLLOWING FILLINGS:

101.

FILLING FOR THREE WAYS TO HEAVEN CAKE

2 TABLESPOONS GELATINE
1 CUP CRUSHED PINEAPPLE
½ CUP THICK RASPBERRY JAM
½ CUP COLD WATER
1 CUP PUREE APRICOTS
¾ CUP CHOPPED PECANS
3 CUPS WHIPPING CREAM

1. SPRINKLE GELATINE OVER COLD WATER AND ALLOW TO STAND FOR 10 MINUTES. DISSOLVE BY PLACING IN A PAN OF HOT WATER.
2. DRAIN JUICE FROM CRUSHED PINEAPPLE.
3. PUREE APRICOTS. EITHER DRIED, COOKED OR CANNED MAY BE USED.
4. WHIP CREAM AND SLOWLY WHIP IN THE DISSOLVED GELATINE. CARE MUST BE TAKEN THAT THE GELATINE DOES NOT BEGIN TO CONGEAL AND GIVE YOU CREAM STRINGS.
5. DIVIDE THE WHIPPED CREAM INTO FOUR PARTS. ADD ONE FRUIT TO EACH PART. THE FOURTH PART IS USED IN STEP 6. FILL THE LAYERS.
6 FROST SIDES AND CENTER OF CAKE WITH PLAIN WHIP CREAM. SPRINKLE THE SIDES OF THE CAKE WITH THE NUTS.

AS THE NAME IMPLIES—THIS IS IT!

102.

TROPICAL, WHAT IS IT?

¼ LB. DRIED APRICOTS
SUGAR
3 FIRM RIPE BANANAS
1 CUP WHIPPED CREAM

1. WASH AND SOAK THE APRICOTS IN WATER FOR 3 HOURS. COOK THEM IN ENOUGH FRESH WATER TO COVER.
2. WHILE APRICOTS ARE STILL HOT SWEETEN WITH AN ABUNDANCE OF SUGAR. THERE SHOULD BE QUITE A BIT OF SYRUP.
3. RUB THE APRICOTS THROUGH A SIEVE AND PLACE IN THE REFRIGERATOR TO CHILL.
4. ADD SLICED BANANAS AND SERVE ICE COLD WITH A GENEROUS AMOUNT OF WHIPPED CREAM.

PLAIN CAKE OR COOKIES MAY ACCOMPANY THIS DESSERT. ALTHOUGH A VERY SIMPLE PUDDING IT IS EXCEEDINGLY TASTY. THIS RECIPE SERVES 4.

✠

NOTES

104.

NOTES

105.

5.

FIRST COURSES

Several of my friends have asked that I include suggestions for the first course. There are countless combinations that are good appetizers. Here are a few to add to your own favorites.

BITTERSWEET PUNCH

                    1 QUART CANNED ORANGE
                    JUICE
               1/3 CUP SUGAR
                    1 TEASPOON ALMOND
                    EXTRACT
                    DASH OF RED COLORING

1. MIX THE JUICE AND EXTRACT TOGETHER. SERVE ICE
   COLD. THE COLOR SHOULD BE A LIGHT BITTERSWEET
   BERRY COLOR.

CANAPE RUSSE

                    TOAST ROUNDS
                    COTTAGE CHEESE
                    RED CAVIAR
                    GREEN PEPPER
                    RADISHES

1. CUT ROUNDS FROM THE BREAD USING A GLASS. TOAST
   AND SPREAD WITH COTTAGE CHEESE.
2. PLACE A THIN RING OF GREEN PEPPER ON TOP OF THE
   CHEESE.
3. IN THE CENTER OF THE CHEESE PLACE $1/2$ TEASPOON OF
   RED CAVIAR.
4. SLICE THE RADISHES INTO THIN ROUNDS AND PLACE
   THEM JUST UNDER THE EDGE OF THE GREEN PEPPER,
   PRESSING SLIGHTLY INTO THE CHEESE IN ORDER THAT
   THEY MAY FORM A COMPLETE CIRCLE AROUND THE
   TOAST RING.

COCKTAIL SAUCE

1 TEASPOON SALT
1/4 TEASPOON PEPPER
1 TEASPOON FINELY
CHOPPED ONION
1 TEASPOON OLIVE OIL
10 DROPS TABASCO SAUCE
2 TABLESPOONS VINEGAR
1 1/2 TEASPOONS WORCESTER-
SHIRE SAUCE
1/2 CUP TOMATO CATSUP

1. MIX ALL INGREDIENTS TOGETHER AND ALLOW TO STAND
IN REFRIGERATOR FOR ONE HOUR BEFORE USING.

THIS IS SUFFICIENT FOR FOUR COCKTAILS.

CHICKEN LIVER, STRASBOURG

1/2 LB. CHICKEN LIVER,
COOKED
1/4 LB. GOOSE LIVER SAUSAGE
FEW GRAINS NUTMEG
2 EGGS, HARD COOKED
JUICE OF 1 LEMON
SALT AND PEPPER TO TASTE

1. GRIND LIVERS VERY FINE.
2. MIX WITH EGGS WHICH HAVE BEEN RUBBED THROUGH
A SIEVE. ADD NUTMEG, SALT, PEPPER AND LEMON JUICE.
ADD A SMALL AMOUNT OF LEMON JUICE AT A TIME,
ADDING THE JUICE TO TASTE.
3. PRESS INTO A SMALL POTTERY BOWL AND PLACE IN RE-
FRIGERATOR UNTIL THOROUGHLY CHILLED.
4. SERVE WITH CRACKERS, WAFERS, AND POTATO CHIPS.

109.

CHILLED CRANBERRY JUICE

5 LB. CRANBERRIES
3 LB. SUGAR
5 QUARTS WATER

1. GRIND CRANBERRIES, ADD SUGAR AND WATER.
2. BRING ONLY TO THE BOILING POINT. REMOVE FROM HEAT, STRAIN AND CHILL.
3. YOU MAY INCREASE SUGAR TO 5 LB. IF A SWEET JUICE IS DESIRED.

THIS WILL MAKE 50 SMALL GLASSES OF JUICE.

CONSOMME TOMATO WITH PARSLEY CREAM

2 QUARTS OF BEEF STOCK
2 CUPS CANNED TOMATOES
1/2 CUP WHIPPED CREAM
1 TABLESPOON PARSLEY

1. BOIL BEEF STOCK WITH TOMATOES. SEASON TO TASTE. STRAIN.
2. WHIP THE CREAM UNTIL VERY STIFF. ADD CHOPPED PARSLEY. MIX TOGETHER. PLACE 1 TEASPOON OF THIS IN EACH CUP AS IT IS SERVED.

THIS MAKES 10 TO 12 SERVINGS. BEEF CONCENTRATE MIGHT BE USED FOR BEEF STOCK OR ONE COULD USE CANNED CONSOMME.

CREAM OF PIMIENTO SOUP

2 TABLESPOONS BUTTER
3 TABLESPOONS FLOUR
1/2 TEASPOON SALT
3 CUPS MILK
4 CUPS CHICKEN STOCK
(FRESH STOCK OR STOCK
MADE BY DISSOLVING 5
BOUILLON CUBES IN 4
CUPS OF BOILING WATER)
1/2 CUP PIMIENTOES
1/2 TEASPOON GRATED ONION
A FEW FLECKS OF PEPPER
(BLACK)

1. MELT BUTTER, ADD FLOUR AND SEASONINGS. BLEND WELL.
2. ADD MILK, MEAT STOCK AND PIMIENTOES THAT HAVE BEEN PUT THROUGH SIEVE.
3. COOK 20 TO 30 MINUTES, STIRRING CONSTANTLY UNTIL MIXTURE THICKENS.

THIS MAKES 10 SERVINGS.

III.

CRABMEAT AND GRAPEFRUIT COCKTAIL

18 SECTIONS OF GRAPEFRUIT
2 CUPS FLAKED CRABMEAT
6 SMALL LETTUCE LEAVES
COCKTAIL SAUCE (PAGE 109)

1. LINE 6 SHERBET OR FISH COCKTAIL CUPS WITH LETTUCE LEAVES. ADD A BIT OF SHREDDED LETTUCE TO THE BOTTOM OF EACH CUP.
2. ARRANGE 3 GRAPEFRUIT SECTIONS AND 1/3 CUP FISH FLAKES IN EACH LETTUCE CUP.
3. SERVE WITH COCKTAIL SAUCE.

THIS RECIPE MAKES 6 COCKTAILS.

✤

FROZEN EGG NOG

                    12 EGGS
                     3 QUARTS OF ICE CREAM
                     6 TEASPOONS VANILLA
                     1 TEASPOON FRESHLY
                       GRATED NUTMEG
                     1 QUART COFFEE CREAM
                     1 QUART MILK

1. BEAT THE EGG YOLKS UNTIL LIGHT.
2. ADD MILK AND CREAM AND BEAT WELL.
3. BREAK THE ICE CREAM INTO SMALL PIECES WITH A FORK AND WHIP THE TWO MIXTURES TOGETHER.
4. ADD VANILLA AND NUTMEG.
5. WHIP THE EGG WHITES UNTIL STIFF AND FROTHY AND FOLD INTO THE EGG NOG.
6. RETURN TO THE FREEZING COMPARTMENT OF YOUR RE-FRIGERATOR TO FREEZE TO A THICKER CONSISTENCY.
7. WHEN READY TO SERVE WHIP ALL TOGETHER TO MIX WELL AND SERVE IN A PUNCH BOWL.

THIS RECIPE SERVES 20 TO 24 GUESTS.
SERVE THIS EGG NOG FROM A PUNCH BOWL FOR A SPE-CIAL PARTY TREAT.

FRUIT CUP MELLOW

1 CUP ROYAL ANNE CHERRIES PITTED AND CUT IN HALF
1 CUP PEACHES, SLICED AND CUT IN QUARTERS
1 CUP BARTLETT PEARS, CUT IN SAME SIZED PIECES AS
   PEACHES
¾ CUP OF VERY SMALL CUBES OF MARSHMALLOWS, ¼"
   CUBES (THIS IS ACCOMPLISHED BY CUTTING WITH SCIS-
   SORS)
1 LEMON, USED AT TIME OF SERVING

1. MIX THE ABOVE INGREDIENTS AND CHILL FOR 3 HOURS
   BEFORE SERVING.
2. WHEN THE FRUIT CUP IS PLACED IN THE SHERBET
   GLASSES CUT THE LEMON INTO 8 SECTIONS AND
   SQUEEZE A SECTION OVER THE TOP OF EACH FRUIT CUP.
   THIS WILL DULL THE SOMEWHAT SWEET FLAVOR OF THE
   MARSHMALLOW AND GIVE A PICK UP TO THE FRUIT CUP
   FLAVOR.

THIS RECIPE SERVES 8.

✤

114.

FRUIT PUNCH

JUICE OF 6 LEMONS
JUICE OF 6 ORANGES
3 TO 4 CUPS SUGAR
2 CUPS CRUSHED PINEAPPLE
2 QUARTS COLD TEA
1 CUP MARASCHINO
CHERRIES, CHOPPED
1 CUP MARASCHINO
CHERRY JUICE
1 PINT GRAPE JUICE
2 QUARTS GINGERALE
3 CUPS WATER

1. BOIL THE PINEAPPLE, WATER AND SUGAR FOR 15 MIN-
UTES. COOL.
2. ADD LEMON, ORANGE AND CHERRY JUICE. ADD CHER-
RIES AND TEA.
3. JUST BEFORE SERVING ADD THE GINGERALE AND GRAPE
JUICE.
4. POUR OVER ICE IN A PUNCH BOWL AND SERVE.

THIS RECIPE WILL SERVE 40 CUPS OF PUNCH.

MULLED CIDER

1 QUART APPLE CIDER
STICK CINNAMON (A SMALL
PIECE WILL BE SUFFICIENT)

1. PLACE A SMALL PIECE OF STICK CINNAMON IN THE
CIDER. HEAT. REMOVE CINNAMON AND SERVE HOT.

YOU MAY USE APPLE JUICE IN THE SAME WAY AND MAY
PREFER THE LESS TANGY FLAVOR OF THE APPLE JUICE TO
THE CIDER. AS A MATTER OF FACT, PLAIN HOT APPLE JUICE
IS VERY GOOD. THIS CIDER MAY BE USED FOR A BEVERAGE
AT A BUFFET SUPPER, WITH DOUGHNUTS OR AS A FIRST
COURSE ON A WINTER EVENING.

✣

116.

NEW ORLEANS CHICKEN GUMBO

2 QUARTS CHICKEN STOCK
1½ CUPS FRESH TOMATOES
(CUT IN SMALL PIECES)
1 CUP FRESH COOKED OR
CANNED OKRA (CUT)
1½ CUPS FINELY DICED
CHICKEN
¼ CUP FINELY CUT GREEN
ONION
½ CUP FINELY CUT GREEN
PEPPER
2½ CUPS COOKED RICE
1 CUP FINELY CUT CELERY
½ CUP BUTTER
MAKE A ROUX BY COOK-
ING TOGETHER FOR 4
MINUTES:
¼ CUP CHICKEN FAT AND
½ CUP FLOUR, STIRRING
CONSTANTLY

1. ADD ROUX TO HOT CHICKEN STOCK. COOK 10 MIN-
UTES.
2. SAUTE ONIONS AND CELERY IN BUTTER 5 MINUTES.
3. ADD GREEN PEPPERS. COOK 4 MINUTES. ADD TOMA-
TOES AND COOK 8 MINUTES.
4. COMBINE ABOVE MIXTURE WITH STOCK. ADD OKRA,
RICE AND CHICKEN. COOK 10 MINUTES LONGER.

THIS SHOULD BE A SLIGHTLY THICKENED SOUP. ADD SALT
AND PEPPER TO TASTE. YOU MAY PLAN ON 12 TO 14 SERV-
INGS, HOWEVER, EVERYONE WILL WISH THEY HAD BEEN
SERVED A DOUBLE PORTION.

117.

POTATO SOUP

1 CARROT
2 POTATOES
HALF MEDIUM SIZED
ONION
1 CUP MILK
SALT AND PEPPER

1. DICE THE POTATO AND CARROT.
2. CHOP THE ONION.
3. PLACE VEGETABLES IN PAN WITH 2$\frac{1}{2}$ CUPS WATER AND COOK UNTIL VEGETABLES ARE TENDER.
4. PUT THIS MIXTURE THROUGH A SIEVE OR VEGETABLE MILL.
5. ADD THE MILK TO THIS PUREE.
6. PLACE IN A DOUBLE BOILER TO HEAT. SEASON.

SERVES 4.

THREE TONE

2 CUPS APPLE JUICE
2 CUPS PEAR JUICE
1 CUP GRAPEFRUIT JUICE

1. MIX JUICES AND CHILL BEFORE SERVING.
THIS WILL SERVE 8 SMALL GLASSES.

118.

NOTES

119.

120.

NOTES

6.

MEATS, FISH AND POULTRY

For everyday meals the usual roasting, broiling or pan frying method is preferred. The following recipes will add variety. After you master the simple steps in making BAKED VEAL LOAF, you will have requests for a repeat performance.

BAKED HONEY HAM, FRUIT SAUCE PIQUANTE

1 10 LB. HAM
1 CUP HONEY
1 CUP BROWN SUGAR
2 CUPS PICKLED PEACH JUICE
½ CUP CIDER VINEGAR
6 WHOLE CLOVES
1 CUP DICED ORANGES
1 CUP DICED PINEAPPLE
1 CUP CUT AND SEEDED GRAPES, WHITE GRAPES PREFERRED

1. WASH HAM AND PLACE FAT SIDE UP IN ROASTER. STICK IN THE 6 CLOVES. POUR THE VINEGAR AND PEACH JUICE OVER THE HAM.
2. RUB WITH THE HONEY THEN THE BROWN SUGAR.
3. BAKE AT 300° F. UNCOVERED FOR 1 HOUR.
4. COVER AND BAKE 2 HOURS. BASTE THE HAM EVERY HALF HOUR.
5. ADD THE DICED FRUITS AND BAKE 1 HOUR OR UNTIL HAM IS TENDER.
6. SERVE THE SLICED HAM WITH THE FRUIT SAUCE FROM THE ROASTER.

124.

BAKED SAVORY TONGUE

PURCHASE 1 PICKLED BEEF
TONGUE
6 CARROTS
1 STALK OF CELERY, ABOUT
6 STEMS
1 MEDIUM SIZED ONION
4 PEPPERCORNS
1/2 TEASPOON SALT
4 SLICES OF LEMON
2 SMALL CANS OF TOMATO
SOUP

1. PUT THE TONGUE IN A KETTLE AND COVER WITH COLD
   WATER, BRING TO A BOIL AND BOIL 8 MINUTES. RE-
   MOVE ANY SCUM THAT MAY HAVE FORMED AND REDUCE
   HEAT, ALLOWING TO SIMMER UNTIL TENDER, 3 TO 4
   HOURS. ALLOW TO COOL SOMEWHAT IN THE STOCK.
   REMOVE FROM LIQUID. SKIN THE TONGUE. REMOVE
   ROOTS.   PLACE THE MEAT IN A ROASTING PAN.
2. SLICE THE CARROTS, CELERY, AND ONIONS.   SPREAD
   OVER THE TONGUE. SPRINKLE THE SALT AND PEPPER-
   CORNS OVER THE MEAT. PLACE THE LEMON SLICES ON
   TOP.
3. MIX THE TOMATO SOUP WITH AN EQUAL AMOUNT OF
   WATER AND POUR OVER THE TONGUE TRYING NOT TO
   DERANGE THE VEGETABLES, ETC., WHICH HAVE BEEN
   PLACED OVER THE MEAT.
4. COVER THE ROASTER AND BAKE AT 375° F. UNTIL THE
   VEGETABLES ARE COOKED.   BASTE FREQUENTLY.
5. SERVE SLICED HOT WITH THE SAUCE FROM THE PAN.
   SHOULD YOU DESIRE TO USE HALF OF THE TONGUE AND
   SAVE THE OTHER HALF FOR COLD SLICED TONGUE,
   MERELY HALVE THE RECIPE.
   THE NUMBER OF SERVINGS DEPENDS ON SIZE OF TONGUE
   AS WELL AS SIZE OF SERVING.

125.

BAKED VEAL LOAF

3 LB. VEAL
2 LB. PORK (HAVE YOUR BUTCHER GRIND THE MEATS TOGETHER FOR YOU)
3 EGGS
2 CUPS MASHED POTATO
I CUP FINE CRACKER CRUMBS (MADE BY ROLLING CRACKERS WITH A ROLLING PIN ON A PASTRY BOARD UNTIL FINELY CRUSHED)
4 TEASPOONS SALT
I MEDIUM SIZED ONION (FINELY GROUND)
¾ CUP BLANCHED ALMONDS

1. MIX ALL WELL TOGETHER WITH YOUR HANDS.
2. PLACE 2 SLICES OF BACON IN BOTTOM OF A ROASTER. FORM A LOAF ON TOP OF THE BACON BY PUTTING THE MEAT IN SHAPE OF A SMALL LOAF OF BREAD. LAY 2 SLICES OF BACON ON TOP OF THE LOAF.
3. NEXT PLACE THE BLANCHED ALMONDS (BLANCHING IS DONE BY PLACING THE ALMONDS IN BOILING WATER FOR A FEW MINUTES, DRAIN OFF THE WATER AND THE BROWN OUTER SHELL WILL SLIDE OFF) ALONG THE MEAT LOAF IN ROWS BETWEEN THE BACON STRIPS THE LENGTH OF THE MEAT LOAF.
4. BAKE IN AN UNCOVERED ROASTER FOR 1½ HOURS AT 375° F.
   ONE HALF OF THIS RECIPE IS SUFFICIENT FOR A FAMILY OF SIX.

126.

BAR B Q PORK AND VEAL TOURNELLE

1 LB. PORK CHOPS, BONE
AND CUT IN 1 INCH
SQUARES
1 LB. VEAL STEAK, CUT IN
1 INCH SQUARES
1½ CUPS DRY BREAD CRUMBS
1 EGG, WELL BEATEN
¼ CUP MILK
SALT AND PEPPER
WOODEN SKEWERS, CAN
BE PURCHASED AT MEAT
MARKET
BAR B Q SAUCE (RECIPE
ON PAGE 145.)

1. MIX THE MILK WITH THE BEATEN EGGS.
2. DIP EACH SQUARE INTO THE EGG WASH, THEN THE CRUMBS.
3. PLACE THE CUBES ON THE SKEWER ALTERNATING PORK AND VEAL.
4. SAUTE IN SKILLET WITH BUTTER OR A SMALL AMOUNT OF BACON FAT UNTIL THE MEAT IS BROWNED EVENLY AND NICELY. A MEDIUM HEAT IS PREFERRED IN ORDER NOT TO BURN THE MEAT.
5. PLACE IN A COVERED ROASTING DISH, PYREX CASSEROLE MAY BE USED. ADD ½ CUP WATER TO THE DRIPPINGS AND MIX WELL. ADD 1 CUP OF THIS MIXTURE TO THE BOTTOM OF THE CASSEROLE.
6. BAKE AT 375° F. FOR 1¼ HOURS. SERVE WITH BAR B Q SAUCE.
THIS RECIPE SERVES 6.

127.

BOONE TAVERN CHICKEN PIE

2 CUPS COOKED CHICKEN, CUBED VERY FINE
4 CUPS CHICKEN FRICASSEE SAUCE
1 CUP CUT MUSHROOMS
3 EGG YOLKS, WELL BEATEN
3 EGG WHITES, BEATEN UNTIL FLUFFY AND STIFF
¾ CUP CHOPPED TOASTED ALMONDS
¼ TEASPOON SALT
¼ TEASPOON PEPPER

1. FOLD BEATEN EGG YOLKS INTO 2 CUPS OF THE FRICASSEE SAUCE. ADD CHICKEN, MUSHROOMS AND SEASONINGS. TASTE AND ADD MORE SALT IF DESIRED.
2. ADD THE ALMONDS. FOLD IN BEATEN EGG WHITES.
3. POUR INTO AN UNBAKED PIE SHELL. BAKE FOR 40 MINUTES AT 350° F.
4. CUT PIE WEDGE PIECES AND SERVE WITH FRICASSEE SAUCE OVER ONE CORNER OF EACH PIECE.

THIS RECIPE SERVES 8.

128.

CHICKEN FRICASSEE SAUCE

3 CUPS CHICKEN BROTH
½ CUP CHICKEN FAT
½ CUP FLOUR
SALT AND PEPPER TO TASTE

1. MAKE A ROUX OF THE FAT AND FLOUR BY ADDING THE FLOUR TO THE HOT MELTED FAT IN A SKILLET. STIR AND COOK FOR 5 MINUTES. ADD HOT BROTH. COOK 10 MINUTES.

✣

BROILED VEAL SWEETBREADS, MUSHROOM SAUCE

1 OR 2 SWEETBREADS
2 TABLESPOONS VINEGAR
1 QUART OF BOILING
 WATER (SALTED)
1 CUP MUSHROOM SAUCE
2 SLICES OF LEMON.

1. PLACE THE SWEETBREADS IN COLD WATER FOR 1 HOUR. THEN DRAIN AND PUT THEM INTO THE BOILING WATER.
2. ADD THE VINEGAR. COOK SLOWLY FOR 20 MINUTES.
3. DRAIN AND PLACE THE SWEETBREADS WHICH HAVE BEEN SPLIT LENGTHWISE IN A WELL BUTTERED BAKING PAN. DOT WITH BUTTER AND SPRINKLE WITH 2 TABLE-SPOONS OF WATER.
4. BROIL FOR 5 MINUTES UNTIL NICELY BROWNED BUT DO NOT ALLOW THE SWEETBREADS TO DRY OUT IN THE BROILING PROCESS.
5. SERVE WITH THE MUSHROOM SAUCE OVER HALF OF EACH SERVING. GARNISH WITH A LEMON SLICE.
RECIPE FOR MUSHROOM SAUCE GIVEN ON PAGE 151.

130.

CHICKEN PINEAPPLE ALMOND CROUSTADE

1 LOAF UNSLICED WHITE BREAD
¾ CUP MELTED BUTTER
2 CUPS COOKED CHICKEN, CUT IN CUBES
3 CUPS CREAM SAUCE
¾ CUP PINEAPPLE (TIDBITS OR CUBES)
¾ CUP SHREDDED ALMONDS

1. TRIM BREAD OF ENTIRE CRUST. CUT SLICES TWO INCHES THICK. CUT THESE IN TWO, THEN WITH A SHARP KNIFE CUT OUT THE CENTERS OF EACH RECTANGLE THUS MAKING A SMALL SHELL. BUTTER EACH WELL WITH MELTED BUTTER. PLACE IN A HOT OVEN TO TOAST (400° F.). REMOVE FROM OVEN AND FILL WITH THE FOLLOWING:
2. MIX CHICKEN AND PINEAPPLE TOGETHER WITH CREAM SAUCE. USE THE RECIPE FOR CHICKEN CREAM SAUCE ON PAGE 147. FILL CENTER OF THE CROUSTADE ALLOWING SOME OF THE FILLING TO RUN OVER THE SIDE OF THE SHELL. SPRINKLE THE TOP WITH A GENEROUS AMOUNT OF THE ALMONDS.

THIS WILL MAKE 6 TO 8 SERVINGS DEPENDING ON THE AMOUNT OF FILLING YOU PREFER.

CHICKEN FLAKES IN BIRDS NEST

4 MEDIUM SIZED IDAHO
POTATOES
5 CUPS OF CHICKEN CREAM
SAUCE (RECIPE ON PAGE
147)
4 CUPS COOKED CHICKEN
(HALF-INCH C U B E S OR
PIECES)
DEEP FAT FOR FRENCH
FRYING POTATO NEST

1. PEEL AND GRATE OR SHRED POTATOES ON A VEGETABLE
   SHREDDER WITH 3/8 INCH ROUND HOLES.
2. LINE A STRAINER (4 INCH DIAMETER AT TOP) WITH THE
   SHREDDED POTATOES, USING ONLY ENOUGH TO THINLY
   COVER THE INSIDE OF STRAINER. PLACE ANOTHER
   STRAINER (2 INCH DIAMETER AT TOP) INSIDE OF THE FIRST
   STRAINER WHICH WILL KEEP THE POTATOES IN PLACE.
3. SET THE STRAINER DOWN IN THE HOT DEEP FAT AND FRY
   UNTIL GOLDEN BROWN. REMOVE AND TAP OR HELP THE
   NEST OUT OF THE BOTTOM STRAINER BY URGING WITH
   THE BLADE OF A KNIFE.
4. ALLOW TO COOL AND REHEAT IN OVEN BEFORE SERVING
   THE CHICKEN FLAKES IN THE SHELL.
5. COMBINE THE CHICKEN FLAKES AND CREAM SAUCE.
   ADD ADDITIONAL SEASONINGS IF DESIRED AND SERVE
   IN THE BIRD NEST.
THIS RECIPE SERVES 8.

THIS CHANGE FROM THE OFTEN SERVED CREAMED CHICKEN
IN PATTY SHELL HAS MET WITH POPULAR ACCLAIM AT
BOONE TAVERN.

132.

COUNTRY CHICKEN PIE

2 CUPS DICED COOKED CHICKEN

½ CUP COOKED CARROTS, DICED 1/3 INCH CUBES

1 CUP FRESH COOKED OR FROZEN COOKED PEAS

¼ CUP FINE CUT ONIONS, SAUTED IN BUTTER

¾ TEASPOON SALT

3 CUPS RICH CHICKEN STOCK

½ CUP CHICKEN FAT

½ CUP FLOUR

1. MAKE A ROUX BY COOKING THE FLOUR IN THE MELTED CHICKEN FAT. THIS IS DONE IN A SKILLET AND COOKED STIRRING 8 MINUTES.
2. HEAT THE CHICKEN STOCK AND ADD THE ROUX. BEAT TO AVOID LUMPING AND COOK FOR 5 MINUTES. ADD THE SEASONINGS.
3. ADD THE VEGETABLES AND CUBED CHICKEN.
4. POUR INTO A BUTTERED CASSEROLE AND TOP WITH COUNTRY CRUST. BAKE AT 375° F. FOR 25 MINUTES.

133.

COUNTRY CRUST

3 EGG YOLKS, BEATEN
UNTIL FLUFFY
3 EGG WHITES, BEATEN UN-
TIL FLUFFY AND STIFF
¾ CUP MILK
1½ CUPS SIFTED FLOUR
2 TEASPOONS BAKING
POWDER
½ TEASPOON SALT
2 TEASPOONS BUTTER

1. SIFT FLOUR, BAKING POWDER AND SALT.
2. WORK THE BUTTER INTO THIS BY RUBBING TOGETHER
WITH THE FINGERS.
3. ADD THE MILK AND EGG YOLKS AND BEAT VIGOROUSLY.
4. FOLD IN THE STIFFLY BEATEN EGG WHITES.
5. SPREAD OVER THE TOP OF THE CASSEROLE AND BAKE.

❖

134.

DUTCH OVEN VEAL CHOPS or TOURNADO OF LAMB

4 LARGE VEAL CHOPS OR
LAMB CHOPS
4 WOODEN SKEWERS
1 CUP FLOUR
1/2 TEASPOON SALT
1/4 TEASPOON PEPPER
1/4 TEASPOON CELERY SALT
3/4 CUP BUTTER OR VEGETABLE
FAT
2 CUPS CREAM

1. REMOVE BONE FROM THE CHOPS. WRAP THE BONED RIB SECTION AROUND THE EYE OF THE CHOP AND SKEWER IN PLACE WITH THE WOODEN STICK.
2. ADD THE SEASONINGS TO THE FLOUR. TOSS THE CHOPS IN THE FLOUR MIXTURE TO COAT.
3. BROWN NICELY BY SAUTEING IN A SKILLET WITH THE BUTTER.
4. REMOVE THE CHOPS AND ADD THE CREAM STIRRING TO PREVENT ANY LUMPS FORMING.
5. PLACE THE CHOPS IN A DUTCH OVEN OR COVERED CASSEROLE AND POUR THE CREAM OVER THEM.
6. BAKE AT 350° F. FOR AT LEAST 2 HOURS. BASTE AND TURN CHOPS IF THE CREAM DOES NOT COVER THEM. BE SURE TO BAKE COVERED. IT MAY BE NECESSARY TO ADD MORE CREAM IN THE BAKING PROCESS. TAKE CARE THAT THE MEAT DOES NOT DRY IN THE CASSEROLE.

ENGLISH HOT POT

1 LB. PORK CHOPS, LEAN
4 SMALL ONIONS
8 OR 9 MEDIUM POTATOES
SALT AND PEPPER

1. BUTTER A DEEP CASSEROLE WELL. INTO THIS SLICE A LAYER OF POTATOES, THEN A LAYER OF ONIONS, FOLLOWED WITH A LAYER OF CUBES OF THE PORK CHOPS. REPEAT, HAVING A LAYER OF POTATOES ON TOP. ADD SALT AND PEPPER TO EACH LAYER.
2. COVER WITH BOILING WATER.
3. BAKE COVERED IN A MODERATE OVEN FOR 2½ TO 3 HOURS. UNCOVER THE CASSEROLE THE LAST HALF HOUR TO BROWN THE TOP.
   THIS IS SUFFICIENT FOR 4 TO 6 PEOPLE. ON A COLD WINTER EVENING THIS SUPPER DISH IS HAPPILY RECEIVED.

✤

136.

NORWEGIAN MEAT BALLS

1 LB. PORK
1½ LB. ROUND STEAK
½ CUP FINELY CUT ONION
1 EGG
1 TABLESPOON CORN-
STARCH
1 TEASPOON SALT
¼ TEASPOON NUTMEG
¼ TEASPOON PEPPER
½ CUP CREAM

1. HAVE BUTCHER GRIND MEATS TOGETHER.
2. MIX IN EGG, ONION, CORNSTARCH AND SEASONINGS.
3. MIX IN CREAM AND SHAPE INTO SMALL BALLS, APPROXI-
MATELY THE SIZE OF A BLUE PLUM.
4. BROWN THESE CAREFULLY IN A SKILLET IN CHICKEN FAT
OR BUTTER. REMOVE FROM SKILLET. STIR INTO THE DRIP-
PINGS 2 TABLESPOONS OF FLOUR. STIR RAPIDLY TO
AVOID BURNING OR LUMPING. ADD 3 CUPS OF THIN
CREAM.
5. POUR THIS OVER MEAT BALLS AND BAKE IN COVERED
DISH FOR 1½ HOURS AT 350° F.

THIS AMOUNT WILL SERVE 12 GUESTS.

THE USE OF AN ELECTRIC MIXER TO WHIP UP THE MIX-
TURE BEFORE SHAPING MEAT BALLS WILL GIVE YOU A
LIGHTER PRODUCT.

137.

PORK CHOPS, SOME TRICKY WAY

4 LEAN PORK CHOPS
½ CUP TOMATO PASTE
½ CUP PARMESAN CHEESE
1 CUP BREAD CRUMBS
2 CUPS CHICKEN STOCK
¾ CUP MUSHROOMS

1. TRIM CHOPS AND BRUSH OVER TO COAT WITH THE TO-MATO PASTE.
2. MIX THE PARMESAN CHEESE WITH THE BREAD CRUMBS.
3. PAT THE BREAD CRUMBS ONTO THE CHOPS.
4. PAN FRY THE CHOPS IN A SKILLET TO BROWN ON BOTH SIDES.
5. PLACE THE CHOPS IN A COVERED CASSEROLE AND ADD A SMALL AMOUNT OF WATER TO PREVENT THEM FROM STICKING TO THE DISH. BAKE FOR 1 HOUR AT 350° F.
6. SERVE WITH A SAUCE MADE BY THICKENING 2 CUPS OF CHICKEN STOCK WITH 2½ TABLESPOONS FLOUR WHICH HAS BEEN SMOOTHED TO A PASTE WITH SOME OF THE COLD STOCK. COOK FOR 5 MINUTES. ADD ¾ CUP OF CUT MUSHROOMS TO THE FINISHED SAUCE.

✤

ROAST CHESTNUT STUFFED TENDERLOIN OF BEEF TORGO

FILET OF BEEF, THE
TENDERLOIN
2 CUPS OF BOILED
CHESTNUTS
1/2 CUP BUTTER
1/4 CUP CREAM
1 CUP CRACKER CRUMBS
1/2 TEASPOON SALT
1/4 TEASPOON PEPPER
1/2 TEASPOON SAGE
2 BANANAS
4 TABLESPOONS CRAN-
BERRY SAUCE

1. TO PREPARE CHESTNUTS: CUT A GASH ON THE FLAT SIDE OF THE NUT. PLACE 1 TABLESPOON COOKING OIL IN A HEAVY PAN. BAKE IN OVEN FOR 8 MINUTES AT 400° F TAKE FROM THE OVEN AND REMOVE SHELLS AND SKIN WITH A KNIFE. COVER WITH BOILING SALTED WATER AND COOK SLOWLY FOR 18 MINUTES. FORCE THE NUTS THROUGH A RICER AND MINCE VERY, VERY FINE, ADD HALF THE BUTTER AND CREAM, THEN ADD THE SALT AND PEPPER. MIX THE REMAINING BUTTER, WHICH HAS BEEN MELTED WITH THE CRUMBS. COMBINE THE TWO MIX-TURES. ADD THE SAGE.
2. SPLICE THE TENDERLOIN LENGTHWISE. FILL WITH THE DRESSING PREPARED ABOVE.
3. PLACE THE TENDERLOIN ON A STRIP OF BACON IN A COVERED ROASTING PAN. PLACE A STRIP OF BACON ON

TOP OF THE MEAT. ADD A CUP OF WATER TO THE BOT-
TOM OF THE PAN.

4. BAKE AT 425° F. FOR 30 MINUTES, BASTING AS IT ROASTS.

5. REMOVE THE MEAT TO SERVING PLATTER AND GARNISH
    WITH THE BAKED BANANA GLACE. A GRAVY IS MADE
    OF THE DRIPPINGS BY THICKENING THE LIQUID WITH
    1 TABLESPOON OF FLOUR MIXED WITH THREE TABLE-
    SPOONS OF COLD WATER AND STIRRED INTO THE DRIP-
    PINGS, COOKING FOR 3 MINUTES.

6. SLICE THE BANANAS LENGTHWISE AND PLACE IN A BUT-
    TERED BAKING DISH. SPREAD A TABLESPOON OF CRAN-
    BERRY SAUCE OVER EACH BANANA AND BAKE FOR 12
    TO 15 MINUTES.

✣

140.

SUSSEX BIRD

1½ LB. SLICE OF VEAL, CUT
AS THIN AS POSSIBLE
6 LARGE SELECT OYSTERS
1½ CUPS CUBED BREAD
1½ TEASPOONS SAGE
1 EGG
¼ CUP MELTED BUTTER
SALT AND PEPPER
¾ CUP CHICKEN STOCK
1 CUP CREAM
1 CUP MILK
3 TABLESPOONS FLOUR

1. SPRINKLE THE VEAL WITH SOME FLOUR AND POUND IT UNTIL IT IS NOT MORE THAN ½ INCH THICK. CUT INTO 6 PIECES, 3 INCHES WIDE.
2. MAKE A DRESSING BY MOISTENING THE BREAD CRUMBS WITH THE CHICKEN STOCK, BEATEN EGG, SALT, PEPPER, MELTED BUTTER AND SAGE.
3. PLACE AN OYSTER ON EACH PIECE OF VEAL AND FILL IN THE SPACE ON BOTH SIDES OF THE OYSTER WITH SOME DRESSING. ROLL THE VEAL UP INTO ROLLS AND FASTEN WITH A TOOTHPICK.
4. PAT FLOUR OVER EACH ROLL AND BROWN IN BUTTER ON TOP OF STOVE.
5. PLACE MEAT IN CASSEROLE. ADD THE FLOUR WHICH HAS BEEN MOISTENED WITH 3 TABLESPOONS OF WATER TO THE DRIPPINGS IN THE SKILLET. ADD THE MILK AND CREAM, STIR WELL TO PREVENT LUMPING AND COOK 3 MINUTES. POUR THIS OVER THE BIRDS AND COVER. ALLOW TO BAKE AT 400° F. FOR 1 TO 1½ HOURS. SERVE WITH THE GRAVY FROM THE CASSEROLE. TURN THE BIRDS TWICE DURING THE BAKING TO PREVENT THEIR DRYING OUT.

141.

THORNWOOD OVEN STEAK

1 LB. LEAN SIRLOIN STEAK
1/2 CUP BACON FAT
1 CUP BREAD CRUMBS
SALT AND PEPPER
FLOUR

1. CUT MEAT INTO 4 STEAKS. DREDGE WITH FLOUR, SALT AND PEPPER. THIS IS ACCOMPLISHED BY MIXING THE SALT AND PEPPER WITH A CUP OF FLOUR AND POUNDING THE MIXTURE INTO THE STEAK BY USING THE EDGE OF A SMALL PLATE.
2. BROWN MEAT IN A SKILLET WITH THE FAT. REMOVE. ADD 2 CUPS OF WATER AND 2 TABLESPOONS OF FLOUR WHICH HAS BEEN SMOOTHED WITH 1/4 CUP COLD WATER. COOK TO THICKEN. POUR OVER THE STEAKS AND PLACE IN A CASSEROLE, COVER AND BAKE AT 350° F. FOR 1 TO 1 1/2 HOURS UNTIL TENDER.
3. REMOVE THE STEAKS FROM THE GRAVY AND TOSS IN THE BREAD CRUMBS. NEXT FRY THE STEAKS IN A SKILLET TO BROWN THE CRUMB COATING.
4. SERVE WITH THE GRAVY FROM THE CASSEROLE.

TOURNADO OF VEAL TORGOR

6 VEAL STEAKS, CUT 1/4 INCH
THICK, WEIGHING 4
OUNCES EACH
6 THIN SLICES BAKED HAM
2 CUPS CREAM

1. TAKE EACH PIECE OF VEAL AND POUND IN ABOUT A TABLESPOON OF FLOUR INTO EACH SLICE USING THE EDGE OF A SAUCER. ADD A BIT OF SALT AND PEPPER TO THE FLOUR.
2. PLACE A SLICE OF HAM ON EACH PIECE OF VEAL AND ROLL UP. HOLD THIS TOGETHER BY INSERTING TWO TOOTHPICKS.
3. PLACE THE ROLLS IN A DUTCH OVEN OR COVERED CASSEROLE. STAND THE ROLLS ON THEIR EDGES. POUR THE CREAM OVER THE MEAT.
4. BAKE AT 350° FOR 1 1/2 HOURS. SERVE WITH SOME OF THE GRAVY OVER EACH TOURNADO. REMOVE THE TOOTHPICKS AT TIME OF SERVING.

THIS RECIPE WILL SERVE 6. ONE COULD CUT THE ROLLS IN HALF AND SERVE MORE IF A SMALLER SERVING IS SATISFACTORY.

VEAL PAPRIKA

2 LB. BONED VEAL CUTLETS
(6 SERVINGS)
1 LARGE ONION (PEELED
AND MINCED)
1 CLOVE GARLIC (USE
SPARINGLY-MINCED)
1¼ CUPS BOILING WATER
2 TABLESPOONS FLOUR
¼ CUP COLD WATER
1 TEASPOON SALT
½ TEASPOON PEPPER
1 TEASPOON PAPRIKA
½ CUP SOUR CREAM

1. HEAT BACON OR VEGETABLE FAT IN PAN.
2. ADD MINCED ONION, GARLIC AND COVER. FRY UNTIL
   ONIONS ARE YELLOW (3 MINUTES).
3. INCREASE HEAT AND ADD THE VEAL THAT HAS BEEN
   TOSSED IN FLOUR. BROWN VEAL EVENLY ON ALL SIDES.
4. ADD SALT, PEPPER, PAPRIKA AND BOILING WATER. RE-
   DUCE HEAT. COVER AND SIMMER GENTLY FOR ONE
   HOUR OR UNTIL VEAL IS TENDER WHEN PIERCED WITH A
   FORK.
5. ADD SOUR CREAM, MIX AND HEAT THOROUGHLY.
6. REMOVE MEAT FROM PAN.
7. DISSOLVE FLOUR IN COLD WATER. POUR INTO CREAM
   MIXTURE AND COOK, STIRRING CONSTANTLY UNTIL
   SMOOTH AND THICK. RETURN VEAL TO SAUCE AND
   HEAT WELL. SERVE.

144.

BAR-B-Q SAUCE

1 QUART OF CATSUP
2 TABLESPOONS MUSTARD
1 TABLESPOON CELERY
SALT
2 WHOLE BAY LEAVES
4 WHOLE CLOVES
¾ CUP BROWN SUGAR
¼ CUP VINEGAR

1. MIX TOGETHER MUSTARD, CELERY SALT AND BROWN SUGAR.
2. ADD VINEGAR, THEN ADD CATSUP.
3. TO THIS MIXTURE ADD BAY LEAVES AND CLOVES.
4. SIMMER FOR TWENTY MINUTES, STIRRING OFTEN TO PREVENT STICKING.
5. REMOVE FROM STOVE AND TAKE OUT BAY LEAVES AND CLOVES.

✣

BROWNED BUTTER RICE

½ CUP BUTTER
1 CUP WASHED RICE
2 CUPS CHICKEN STOCK

1. BROWN THE BUTTER IN A COVERED SKILLET.
2. ADD THE RICE AND COOK TO BROWN RICE AS IT IS STIRRED.
3. ADD THE CHICKEN STOCK ¼ CUP AT A TIME AS THE RICE COOKS AND ABSORBS THE STOCK. SALT AND PEPPER TO TASTE.

THIS RICE IS EXCELLENT SERVED WITH CREAMED CHICKEN OR FISH DISHES. CAN ALSO BE USED AS A POTATO SUBSTITUTE.

✢

146.

CAPER GRAVY

2 TABLESPOONS BUTTER
3 TABLESPOONS FLOUR, SIFTED
1/8 TEASPOON PEPPER
1 1/2 CUPS DRIPPINGS FROM ROAST LEG OF LAMB, NOT MELTED FAT
1/2 CUP RICH CREAM
1/2 CUP CAPERS, DRAINED

1. MAKE A ROUX OF THE BUTTER AND FLOUR BY STIRRING TOGETHER IN A SKILLET COOKING FOR 2 MINUTES.
2. POUR THE DRIPPINGS INTO THE ROUX AND STIR TO MIX WELL AND PREVENT LUMPING. COOK 5 MINUTES.
3. ADD THE PEPPER AND CREAM.
4. ADD THE CAPERS.
   THE FLOWER OF THE CAPER BUSH ADDS MUCH TO THE TASTINESS OF A ROAST SHOULDER OR LEG OF LAMB.

CHICKEN CREAM SAUCE

6 CUPS CHICKEN STOCK
1 CUP CHICKEN FAT
1 CUP FLOUR
SALT AND PEPPER

1. MAKE A ROUX BY COMBINING FLOUR AND FAT IN A HEAVY SAUCE PAN OR SKILLET. COOK FOR 5 MINUTES, STIRRING CONSTANTLY TO PREVENT STICKING.
2. HEAT CHICKEN STOCK. ADD ROUX AND COOK 10 MINUTES TO THICKEN.
3. SEASON WITH SALT AND PEPPER AS DESIRED.

147.

COTTAGE CHEESE WHIP

1 CUP COTTAGE CHEESE
1 CUP WHIPPED CREAM
2 TABLESPOONS HORSE-
RADISH, PREPARED FRESH
OR BOTTLED MOIST TYPE
1/4 TEASPOON PEPPER
1/4 TEASPOON SALT
1 TABLESPOON LEMON JUICE

1. MIX THE WHIPPED CREAM WITH THE CHEESE.
2. MIX THE OTHER INGREDIENTS WELL AND COMBINE THE
TWO MIXTURES.
THE DEGREE OF SHARPNESS YOU DESIRE WILL BE DETER-
MINED BY THE AMOUNT OF HORSERADISH YOU USE.
THIS IS QUITE ELEGANT WITH COLD OR HOT BAKED HAM
OR SLICED COLD TONGUE.

CRUMB DRESSING

3 CUPS FRESH BREAD
CRUMBS
1/2 TEASPOON SAGE
1/2 TEASPOON SALT
1/2 TEASPOON PEPPER
1/2 CUP MINCED FINE ONIONS
1/4 TEASPOON CELERY SALT
1/4 CUP BUTTER

1. MIX ALL INGREDIENTS TOGETHER AND PLACE IN THE
OVEN TO TOAST. A TEMPERATURE OF 350° F. CAN BE
USED. THIS TOASTED DRESSING IS DELICATE AND DE-
LICIOUS.

148.

DUMPLINGS

2 CUPS FLOUR
1 CUP CREAM
5 TEASPOONS BAKING
POWDER
2 EGGS WELL BEATEN
¾ TEASPOON SALT

1. SIFT FLOUR AND BAKING POWDER AND SALT.
2. ADD EGGS AND CREAM AND BEAT WELL TOGETHER.
3. DROP BY SPOONFULS IN A STEAMER WHICH HAS BEEN WELL BUTTERED BOTH BOTTOM AND SIDES WHERE THE DUMPLINGS MIGHT TOUCH IN RISING.
4. PLACE OVER THE STEAM AND COOK FOR 15 MINUTES.

A STEAMER MAY BE IMPROVISED BY USING A COLANDER WHICH EITHER FITS DOWN INTO ANOTHER KETTLE WITH-OUT TOUCHING THE BOTTOM WHERE THE WATER WILL BE BOILING TO MAKE THE STEAMER OPERATE OR ELSE THE FEET ON THE COLANDER WILL PREVENT THE DUMPLINGS FROM TOUCHING THE BOILING WATER. COVER SECURE-LY AND ALLOW TO COOK AS ABOVE. THE BUTTERING OF THE BOTTOM AND SIDES OF STEAMER IS TO PREVENT THE DUMPLINGS FROM STICKING.

149.

LEMON CLOVES SAUCE

1 CUP WATER
1 CUP SUGAR
1/2 CUP LEMON JUICE
    RIND OF TWO LEMONS
12 WHOLE CLOVES
2 TABLESPOONS CORN-
    STARCH

1. MIX SUGAR WITH CORNSTARCH. ADD WATER. COOK IN DOUBLE BOILER UNTIL THE CONSISTENCY OF A THICK SAUCE.
2. ADD CLOVES, LEMON JUICE AND RIND. COOL.
THIS SAUCE MAY BE SERVED WITH BAKED HAM OR AS A PUDDING SAUCE.

MINT SAUCE

1 CUP VINEGAR
1 CUP SUGAR
1/4 TEASPOON SALT
1/2 CUP MINT LEAVES

1. BOIL SUGAR, SALT AND VINEGAR TO MAKE A SYRUP. BOIL UNTIL IT TESTS 235° F. WITH A CANDY THERMOMETER OR UNTIL IT RUNS OFF THE EDGE OF A SPOON THE CONSISTENCY OF HONEY.
2. POUR SYRUP OVER THE FRESHLY CHOPPED MINT LEAVES AND COVER. ALLOW TO COOL.

150.

MUSHROOM SAUCE

I CUP OF CHICKEN FRICAS-
SEE SAUCE (SEE PAGE 129)
I CUP BUTTON MUSHROOMS
2 TABLESPOONS BUTTER

1. SAUTE THE MUSHROOMS IN THE BUTTER.
2. ADD THE FRICASSEE SAUCE AND ALLOW TO COME TO A BOIL.

NOODLES

2 EGGS
1/2 TEASPOON SALT
1 1/4 CUPS FLOUR

I BEAT EGGS SLIGHTLY. ADD SALT AND FLOUR. THIS MAKES A STIFF DOUGH.
2. KNEAD AND TOSS ON A FLOURED BOARD. ROLL AS THIN AS POSSIBLE. SPRINKLE WITH FLOUR. FOLD IN LAYERS ABOUT 2 INCHES WIDE, THEN SLICE VERY THIN AND SHAKE OUT EACH STRIP SEPARATELY. COOK UNTIL TENDER IN BOILING SALTED WATER FOR 20 MINUTES.

POTATO DUMPLINGS

3 OR 4 BOILED POTATOES
CUBES OF WHITE BREAD (3
SLICES CUT IN ½ INCH
CUBES)
1 EGG
1 TEASPOON OF BAKING
POWDER
1 CUP FLOUR
¾ CUP CHOPPED ONIONS

1. BROWN BREAD CUBES IN BUTTER.
2. GRATE THE POTATOES.
3. ADD ONIONS AND BREAD CUBES AND BEATEN EGG TO POTATOES.
4. ADD FLOUR WHICH HAS BEEN SIFTED WITH BAKING POWDER TO ABOVE MIXTURE AND STIR WELL. THIS IS A STIFF MIXTURE.
5. SHAPE INTO BALLS HAVING A BREAD CUBE IN CENTER OF EACH BALL.
6. DROP INTO BOILING SALTED WATER AND BOIL FOR 8 MINUTES COVERED. REMOVE AND SERVE AT ONCE WITH GRAVY.

THESE DUMPLINGS ARE PARTICULARLY GOOD SERVED WITH ROAST LOIN OF PORK, POT ROAST OF BEEF, OR ANY RAGOUT TYPE OF DISH.

POTATO PANCAKES

3 EGGS
5 LARGE GRATED POTATOES
(RAW)
3 TABLESPOONS MILK
2 TABLESPOONS FLOUR
1/2 TEASPOON SALT

1. BEAT THE EGGS AND MIX INTO THE POTATOES.
2. SIFT FLOUR AND SALT INTO POTATOES, ADD MILK.
3. BEAT TOGETHER.
4. FRY IN A SKILLET IN BACON FAT OR BUTTER. SPOON ABOUT 2 TABLESPOONS BATTER PER PANCAKE INTO HOT GREASE. COOK 2 MINUTES, TURN AND COOK OTHER SIDE 2 MINUTES.
5. SERVE IMMEDIATELY WITH BUTTER AND IF YOU LIKE (AS I DO) A SPRINKLING OF SUGAR.

✤

153.

RAW CRANBERRY RELISH

1 QUART OF CRANBERRIES
1 APPLE
2 PEARS
2½ CUPS SUGAR
2 ORANGES

1. PUT THE CRANBERRIES AND THE FRUIT INCLUDING THE PEELINGS THROUGH THE FOOD CHOPPER.
2. ADD THE SUGAR AND ALLOW TO SET FOR 3 HOURS.

THIS RELISH IS DELICIOUS WITH CHICKEN AND TURKEY AND CAN ALSO BE USED WITH CELERY IN A JELLIED CRANBERRY SALAD.

IN MAKING A CRANBERRY SALAD MERELY MAKE UP A PINT OF STRAWBERRY GELATINE DESSERT POWDER AND WHEN COOL ADD 2 CUPS OF CRANBERRY RELISH AND ONE CUP OF FINELY CUT CELERY.

✤

154.

RHUBARB CONSERVE

1 CUP CANNED PINEAPPLE
CUT IN PIECES
6 CUPS RHUBARB, CUT IN 1
INCH PIECES
SUGAR
2 ORANGES, ALSO THE RIND
1 CUP BLANCHED ALMONDS,
SPLIT IN HALF

1. COOK THE PINEAPPLE AND RHUBARB TOGETHER UNTIL SOFT. THE MOISTURE FROM THE WASHED RHUBARB IS SUFFICIENT FOR THE COOKING DOWN PROCESS. STIR TO PREVENT SCORCHING.
2. MEASURE COOKED FRUIT AND USE AN EQUAL AMOUNT OF SUGAR.
3. REMOVE WHITE MEMBRANE OF THE ORANGE PEELING AND CUT IN SMALL PIECES. COOK THE RIND IN 1 CUP WATER FOR 3 MINUTES, CHANGE THE WATER AND RE-COOK 3 MINUTES.
4. ADD THE RIND AND ORANGE JUICE TO THE FRUIT AND SUGAR. BRING TO BOILING POINT AND THEN SIMMER FOR 40 MINUTES.
5. ADD ALMONDS AND COOK FOR 15 MINUTES.

THIS SHOULD MAKE 8 GLASSES OF CONSERVE. IT IS WELL LIKED AS AN ACCOMPANIMENT TO ROAST MEATS.

SOUTHERN BREAD DRESSING

3 CUPS CORNBREAD,
BROKEN IN PIECES
2 CUPS WHITE BREAD,
BROKEN IN PIECES
1/3 TABLESPOON GROUND
SAGE
1/4 TEASPOON BLACK PEPPER
2 CUPS RICH CHICKEN
STOCK
1/2 CUP MINCED FINE ONION

1. MIX ALL TOGETHER.
2. PLACE IN A BAKING PAN AND BAKE AT 350° F. FOR 35
MINUTES.

THIS IS THE DRESSING THE NORTHERNERS WONDER HOW
THE SOUTHERNERS MAKE AND THE SOUTHERNERS WON-
DER WHY THE NORTHENERS DON'T KNOW HOW.

✤

156.

SPANISH SAUCE

2 TABLESPOONS FINE CUT HAM
2 TABLESPOONS CUT ONION
2/3 CUP TOMATOES (CANNED)
1 TABLESPOON FLOUR
2 TABLESPOONS CUT CELERY
2 TABLESPOONS CUT GREEN PEPPER
3 TABLESPOONS BUTTER
SALT AND PEPPER

1. MELT BUTTER IN THE SKILLET AND SAUTE ALL THE VEGE-
TABLES AND HAM TOGETHER FOR A FEW MINUTES. THE
HAM USED IS COOKED HAM.
2. MIX THE FLOUR WITH A TABLESPOON OF COLD WATER
TO FORM A SMOOTH PASTE.
3. ADD THE TOMATOES AND THE FLOUR PASTE TO THE
VEGETABLES AND COOK FOR FIVE MINUTES STIRRING TO
PREVENT STICKING OR LUMPING.
4. SEASON TO TASTE . . . OTHER SEASONINGS MAY BE
ADDED IF YOU DESIRE A HOTTER TYPE SAUCE. WHEN
SERVED WITH THE FISH OMELET THE LESS HIGHLY SEA-
SONED SAUCE IS PREFERRED.

THIS RECIPE IS FOR 2 OR 3 SERVINGS.

157.

BROILED CHINOOK SALMON

4 SERVINGS OF FRESH SAL-
MON, PURCHASED AT THE
MARKET AS FILETS AND CUT
INTO DESIRED SIZE SERV-
INGS
BOILING SALTED WATER
¾ CUP BUTTER
JUICE OF LEMON

1. PREPARE FISH AND COOK AS FOR BROILED LAKE TROUT.
2. BROWN BUTTER SLIGHTLY IN A SKILLET AND ADD LEMON
   JUICE. SERVE OVER THE FISH.
3. THIS IS A RICH RATHER DRY FISH AND REQUIRES BAST-
   ING AS IT BROILS AND SUFFICIENT LEMON BUTTER WHEN
   SERVED.

❖

158.

BROILED LAKE TROUT, ALMOND SAUCE

4 SERVINGS OF LAKE TROUT,
BUY FILETS CUT INTO DE-
SIRED SIZE SERVINGS AT
THE MARKET
¾ CUP BUTTER
JUICE OF 1 LEMON
¼ CUP MINCED FINE RIND OF
LEMON
½ CUP CUT TOASTED
ALMONDS
PINCH OF SALT IN WATER

1. PLACE THE FISH IN SKILLET WITH JUST ENOUGH BOILING
WATER TO COVER. COOK 12 MINUTES.
2. NEXT REMOVE FISH AND PLACE ON A PAN. BUTTER TOPS
OF FISH WELL AND SPRINKLE WITH SALT AND PEPPER.
PLACE UNDER THE BROILER AND BROIL FOR 5 MINUTES.
BASTE FISH IF NECESSARY TO PREVENT DRYING DURING
THE BROILING PROCESS.
3. SPRINKLE THE TOP WITH PAPRIKA AND MORE BUTTER AND
RETURN TO THE BROILER TO BROWN.
4. SERVE WITH THE REMAINING BUTTER WHICH HAS BEEN
MELTED AND BROWNED SLIGHTLY IN A SMALL SKILLET.
TO THIS BUTTER ADD THE LEMON JUICE AND A PART
OF THE MINCED LEMON RIND AS WELL AS THE ALMONDS.

BROILED RED SNAPPER, LEMON BUTTER

PURCHASE FRESH RED
SNAPPER ALLOWING 1
POUND OF FILETED FISH
FOR THREE SERVINGS
BOILING SALTED WATER
¼ LB. BUTTER
JUICE AND CHOPPED RIND
OF ONE LEMON

1. WASH THE FISH AND PLACE IN A SKILLET OF BOILING SALTED WATER. WATER LEVEL SHOULD JUST BARELY COVER THE FISH.
2. ALLOW TO SIMMER FOR 12 MINUTES.
3. PLACE ON A PAN, SPREAD HALF OF THE BUTTER OVER THE FISH AND ALLOW TO BROIL FOR 5 MINUTES. BASTE AS FISH BROILS TO AVOID DRYING.
4. SAUTE THE CHOPPED FINE LEMON RIND AND THE REMAINING BUTTER FOR A FEW MINUTES. ADD THE LEMON JUICE AND SERVE OVER THE FISH.
A GENEROUS DASH OF PAPRIKA OVER THE FISH AS IT BROILS WILL GIVE A NICELY BROWNED FINISH.

160.

FRIED FILET OF HADDOCK, TARTAR SAUCE

PURCHASE FILET OF HAD-
DOCK, FRESH OR FROZEN
DEEP FAT FOR FRYING PUR-
POSES, USE HYDROGENAT-
ED SHORTENING IN A DEEP
SKILLET, 4 INCHES
1 CUP SIFTED FLOUR
1 TEASPOON BAKING
POWDER
2 TABLESPOONS CORNMEAL
1/2 TEASPOON SALT
2 EGGS, BEATEN LIGHT
1/4 CUP MILK

1. SIFT FLOUR, BAKING POWDER, MEAL AND SALT.
2. ADD THE MILK TO THE BEATEN EGG YOLKS AND MIX
   WELL.
3. DIP THE FILET AS CUT FOR INDIVIDUAL SERVING INTO THE
   EGG WASH THEN THE DRY BATTER, COATING WELL.
4. FRY IN THE DEEP FAT WHICH HAS BEEN HEATED TO 370° F.
   FOR 4 TO 6 MINUTES. THE FISH SHOULD BE NICELY
   BROWNED. REMOVE BY LIFTING AND DRAINING ON A
   PIECE OF PAPER TOWEL.
5. SERVE WITH TARTAR SAUCE.

TARTAR SAUCE

1 TABLESPOON LEMON JUICE
1 CUP MAYONNAISE
¼ TABLESPOON FINELY
CHOPPED ONION
1 TABLESPOON CHOPPED
STUFFED OLIVE
1 TABLESPOON CHOPPED
PICKLE

1. COMBINE ALL INGREDIENTS.

TAVERN HUSH PUPPY

1 CUP WHITE CORN MEAL
1 EGG
¼ TEASPOON BAKING SODA
½ TEASPOON BAKING
POWDER
½ CUP BUTTERMILK
½ TEASPOON SALT
½ CUP ONION GRATED

1. SIFT SALT, BAKING POWDER, AND CORN MEAL.
2. MIX SODA WITH BUTTERMILK.
3. MIX ABOVE TWO MIXTURES.
4. ADD BEATEN EGG AND MIX WELL.
5. ADD GRATED ONIONS.
6. SHAPE INTO SMALL BALLS AND DROP INTO DEEP FAT. FRY
UNTIL GOLDEN BROWN.

162.

164.

165.

7.

PIES

Of greatest importance in creating a pie is the quality of pastry. A "good hand" at pastry requires some practice to produce the desired flakiness. Try these recipes for "real eating goodness."

BOONE TAVERN CHEESE PIE

2 TEASPOONS CORNSTARCH
6 TABLESPOONS SUGAR
1/8 TEASPOON SALT
3 EGG YOLKS
1 CUP WATER
1 TABLESPOON PLAIN GELATINE
2 TABLESPOONS COLD WATER
2 CUPS COTTAGE CHEESE
4 TABLESPOONS LEMON JUICE
GRATED RIND OF 2 LEMONS
1 CUP WHIPPED CREAM
3 EGG WHITES
1 BAKED PIE SHELL
1/4 CUP GRAHAM CRACKER CRUMBS MIXED WITH 2 TABLESPOONS SUGAR AND 1/2 TEASPOON CINNAMON

168.

1. SPRINKLE GELATINE OVER 2 TABLESPOONS COLD WATER. ALLOW TO STAND FOR 5 MINUTES.
2. MIX THE CORNSTARCH, 6 TABLESPOONS SUGAR AND SALT WITH 1 CUP WATER. ADD TO BEATEN EGG YOLKS.
3. COOK IN A DOUBLE BOILER UNTIL IT THICKENS.
4. ADD THE GELATINE AND STIR TO DISSOLVE.
5. REMOVE FROM FIRE AND COOL UNTIL THICK.
6. ADD LEMON JUICE AND RIND. FOLD IN COTTAGE CHEESE.
7. FOLD IN STIFFLY BEATEN CREAM.
8. FOLD IN STIFFLY BEATEN EGG WHITES.
9. POUR INTO A BAKED PIE SHELL.
10. SPRINKLE THE GRAHAM CRACKER MIXTURE OVER THE TOP OF THE PIE.
11. CHILL THOROUGHLY IN REFRIGERATOR AND SERVE WITH WHIPPED CREAM.

✤

CHOCOLATE PIE, TORGO

3 CUPS OF BROWN SUGAR
(PACK THE CUP WHEN
MEASURING)
1/2 CUP BUTTER
3 EGGS
1/2 CUP COFFEE CREAM
1 TEASPOON VANILLA
1 SQUARE OF MELTED
CHOCOLATE

1. CREAM THE BUTTER AND THE SUGAR TOGETHER UNTIL WELL BLENDED.
2. ADD THE EGGS AND VANILLA AND BEAT ALL TOGETHER.
3. ADD THE CREAM AND MIX.
4. ADD THE MELTED CHOCOLATE AND BLEND TOGETHER.
5. POUR INTO AN UNBAKED PASTRY SHELL, PAGE 173.
6. BAKE AT 350° FOR 30 MINUTES THEN REDUCE TEMPERATURE TO 200° F. FOR 50 MINUTES.
7. WHEN PIE IS COOLED SERVE WITH WHIPPED CREAM. THIS RECIPE MAKES ONE 9 INCH PIE, SERVES EIGHT.

DREAM PIE

¾ CUP SUGAR
3 EGG WHITES BEATEN STIFF
1 TEASPOON VINEGAR
1 TEASPOON VANILLA

1. BEAT EGG WHITES UNTIL FROTHY, SLOWLY ADD THE SUGAR AND CONTINUE BEATING.
2. ADD THE VINEGAR AND VANILLA. CONTINUE TO BEAT UNTIL STIFF AND GLOSSY.
3. SPREAD IN A GREASED 9 INCH PAN. BE SURE TO SHAPE THE WHITES OVER THE BOTTOM OF THE PAN AND WITH A SPATULA POINT UP THE SIDES OF THE PAN JUST A BIT.
4. BAKE 1 HOUR AND 15 MINUTES AT 250° F.
5. REMOVE FROM OVEN AND COOL.

FILL WITH FOLLOWING FILLING:

171.

FILLING FOR DREAM PIE

4 EGG YOLKS
½ CUP SUGAR
6 TABLESPOONS LEMON
   JUICE
1 TEASPOON GELATINE
2 TABLESPOON COLD
   WATER
4 EGG WHITES BEATEN STIFF
¼ CUP SUGAR

1. PLACE THE BEATEN EGG YOLKS MIXED WITH THE SUGAR
   AND LEMON JUICE IN A DOUBLE BOILER AND COOK FOR
   8 MINUTES TO THICKEN.
2. SPRINKLE GELATINE OVER 2 TABLESPOONS COLD WATER
   AND ALLOW TO STAND FOR 5 MINUTES.
3. ADD THE GELATINE TO THE HOT COOKED MIXTURE.
4. BEAT THE EGG WHITES UNTIL STIFF AND BEAT IN THE
   SUGAR. ADD TO THE ABOVE MIXTURE AFTER IT HAS HAD
   A CHANCE TO REACH ROOM TEMPERATURE.
5. FILL PIE SHELL AND PLACE ALL IN THE REFRIGERATOR TO
   COOL AND SET.

172.

PIE CRUST

¾ CUP LARD
2 CUPS FLOUR
4 DESSERT SPOONS OF ICE
   WATER, THIS IS APPROXI-
   MATELY ⅛ CUP
½ TEASPOON SALT
2 TABLESPOONS CREAM

1. MIX FLOUR, SALT AND LARD TOGETHER BY RUBBING BE-
   TWEEN THE FINGER TIPS. THIS WILL PRODUCE A SOFT
   AND RATHER DAMP MIXTURE.
2. ADD WATER AND MIX.
3. SEPARATE INTO 2 PARTS. TOSS ON WELL FLOURED
   BOARD. DUST ROLLING PIN WITH FLOUR AND ROLL AS
   THIN AS POSSIBLE TO HOLD TOGETHER.

THE CREAM IS USED TO MOISTEN THE TOP OF THE TOP
CRUST IN A 2 CRUST PIE OR IN A 1 CRUST PIE. THIS PRO-
DUCES A FLAKY, BROWNED CRUST. BAKE AT 450° F. FOR
12 TO 15 MINUTES FOR A SINGLE SHELL.

173.

EGG NOG PIE

2 CUPS MILK
¾ CUP SUGAR
1 TABLESPOON CORN-
STARCH
1 TABLESPOON GELATINE
¼ CUP COLD WATER
1 TABLESPOON VANILLA
¼ TEASPOON SALT
4 EGGS
4 TABLESPOONS SUGAR
½ PINT WHIPPED CREAM
2 TEASPOONS FRESHLY
GRATED NUTMEG, USE THE
WHOLE NUTMEG AND
GRATE ON SMALL GRATER
1 CUP CHOPPED ALMONDS
OR PECANS

1. SPRINKLE THE GELATINE OVER THE COLD WATER.
2. PLACE THE MILK IN A DOUBLE BOILER AND ALLOW TO HEAT.
3. MIX THE SUGAR AND CORNSTARCH AND SALT TO-GETHER, ADD TO THE HOT MILK. STIR TO PREVENT LUMP-ING. BEAT EGG YOLKS UNTIL CREAMY AND ADD. COOK

174.

TO THICKEN, ABOUT 10 MINUTES BEATING OCCASION-
ALLY WITH ROTARY EGG BEATER.

4. REMOVE FROM HEAT AND ADD VANILLA AND SOF-
TENED GELATINE. STIR TO DISSOLVE. PLACE FILLING
TO COOL.

5. WHEN FILLING IS COLD, ROOM TEMPERATURE, BEAT EGG
WHITES UNTIL FROTHY STIFF AND BEAT IN THE 4 TABLE-
SPOONS OF SUGAR. CONTINUE TO BEAT THE WHITES
TO FORM A STIFF MIXTURE. FOLD INTO THE COOKED
FILLING.

6. POUR THE MIXTURE INTO A BAKED PIE SHELL. SPRINKLE
THE GRATED NUTMEG OVER THE TOP. PLACE THE PIE
IN THE REFRIGERATOR UNTIL THOROUGHLY CHILLED.

7. SERVE EACH PIECE OF PIE TOPPED GENEROUSLY WITH
WHIPPED CREAM AND SPRINKLED WITH 1 TEASPOON OF
CHOPPED NUTS.

✛

JAMBOREE PIE

½ CUP SUGAR
½ CUP BUTTER
½ CUP BLACKBERRY JAM
2 EGG YOLKS
2 EGG WHITES
½ TEASPOON VANILLA

1. CREAM BUTTER AND SUGAR.
2. ADD BEATEN EGG YOLKS AND VANILLA, THEN ADD JAM AND MIX WELL.
3. FOLD IN THE STIFFLY BEATEN EGG WHITES.
4. BAKE IN AN UNCOOKED 8 OR 10 INCH PIE SHELL. THE BAKING PROCESS WILL ALLOW MIXTURE TO RISE TO NOBLE HEIGHTS, HOWEVER AFTER THE PIE COOLS IT WILL SETTLE TO NORMAL DEPTH. BAKE AT 350° F. FOR 45 MINUTES.
5. REMOVE FROM OVEN AND COOL. FILL PIE SHELL WITH CREAM FILLING AND TOP WITH A MERINGUE.

CREAM FILLING FOR JAMBOREE PIE

2 CUPS MILK
¾ CUP SUGAR
5 TABLESPOONS FLOUR
¼ TEASPOON SALT
4 WELL BEATEN EGG YOLKS
1 TEASPOON VANILLA

1. SCALD MILK IN DOUBLE BOILER.
2. MIX SUGAR, FLOUR AND SALT. ADD TO MILK. COOK FOR 15 MINUTES.
3. ADD EGG YOLKS. COOK 5 MINUTES LONGER.
4. ADD VANILLA.

MERINGUE

4 EGG WHITES
½ CUP SUGAR
½ TEASPOON VINEGAR

1. BEAT EGG WHITES UNTIL FROTHY.
2. ADD SUGAR AND CONTINUE BEATING. ADD VINEGAR AND BEAT UNTIL GLOSSY AND STIFF.
3. SPREAD OVER THE FILLING AND BAKE AT 300° F. FOR 15 MINUTES.

177.

KENTUCKY LEMON PIE

1 UNBAKED PIE SHELL
6 EGGS
JUICE OF 2 LEMONS
1½ CUPS CORN SYRUP
¾ CUP SUGAR
⅛ CUP BUTTER
RIND OF 1 LEMON
1 TEASPOON CORNSTARCH

1. BEAT EGGS WELL.
2. ADD SYRUP. MIX WELL.
3. MIX CORNSTARCH WITH THE SUGAR. ADD TO THE SYRUP MIXTURE. ADD LEMON JUICE AND GRATED RIND.
4. ADD MELTED BUTTER. BEAT TOGETHER UNTIL WELL MIXED.
5. POUR INTO UNBAKED PIE SHELL. BAKE ON LOWER SHELF OF OVEN AT 375° F. FOR 15 MINUTES THEN REDUCE THE TEMPERATURE TO 300° F. FOR 40 MINUTES OR UNTIL PIE IS SET.

✤

LIME CHIFFON PIE

1 PACKAGE LEMON
   GELATINE DESSERT
3 EGG YOLKS, 4 EGG
   WHITES
   PINCH SALT
1/2 CUP FROZEN LIMEADE
   (UNDILUTED)
1/2 CUP SUGAR
4 EGG WHITES
1/2 CUP SUGAR
   CHOCOLATE SHOT

1. DISSOLVE THE LEMON GELATINE IN 1 CUP BOILING WATER. COOL TO TEPID.
2. BEAT THE EGG YOLKS, ADD SALT, 1/2 CUP SUGAR AND LIME JUICE. MIX WELL AND COOK IN TOP OF DOUBLE BOILER UNTIL THICKENED.
3. REMOVE FROM FIRE AND ADD TEPID GELATINE MIXTURE. BLEND.
4. ALLOW THIS MIXTURE TO COOL UNTIL THICKENED CONSIDERABLY BUT NOT CONGEALED.
5. WHIP THE EGG WHITES UNTIL FROTHY AND ADD THE 1/2 CUP SUGAR AND CONTINUE TO WHIP UNTIL THE MIXTURE STANDS IN PEAKS.
6. FOLD THE EGG WHITES INTO THE THICKENED GELATINE MIXTURE.
7. POUR FILLING INTO A BAKED PIE SHELL, PAGE 173, AND TOP GENEROUSLY WITH CHOCOLATE SHOT.
8. ALLOW PIE TO CHILL FOR AN HOUR BEFORE SERVING.

179.

MOCHA MAPLE CREAM PIE

1 BAKED PIE SHELL
5 TABLESPOONS FLOUR
¾ CUP BROWN SUGAR
2 CUPS MILK
3 EGGS
½ TEASPOON SALT
1½ TEASPOON MAPLE
FLAVORING
2 CUPS FRESH COFFEE
½ CUP SUGAR
3 TABLESPOONS CORN-
STARCH

1. SCALD MILK IN A DOUBLE BOILER.
2. MIX FLOUR AND SUGAR.
3. ADD TO THE SCALDED MILK STIRRING IN ORDER TO PREVENT LUMPING.
4. STIR FREQUENTLY AND COOK FOR 12 MINUTES.
5. ADD EGG YOLKS BEATEN UNTIL LIGHT. REDUCE HEAT BELOW DOUBLE BOILER DURING THIS PROCESS.
6. COOK 3 MINUTES. ADD FLAVORING AND SALT.
7. ALLOW TO COOL 15 MINUTES.
8. WHILE ABOVE MIXTURE COOLS COOK MOCHA JELLY, USING THE FOLLOWING METHOD:
9. HEAT COFFEE TO SCALDING POINT IN DOUBLE BOILER.
10. ADD SUGAR AND CORNSTARCH WHICH HAVE BEEN WELL BLENDED.
11. STIR WHILE COOKING, IF LUMPS OCCUR BEAT WITH ROTARY BEATER UNTIL SMOOTH.
12. COOK FOR 12 MINUTES. REMOVE FROM FIRE AND COOL 15 MINUTES. (CONTINUED NEXT PAGE.)

180.

13. YOUR CREAM FILLING HAS NOW COOLED SUFFICIENTLY TO POUR INTO BAKED SHELL. ALLOW FILLING TO COOL IN SHELL 15 MINUTES.
14. SPREAD MOCHA JELLY OVER CREAM FILLING.
15. ALLOW JELLY TO SET DURING THE PREPARATION OF THE MERINGUE.
16. MERINGUE IS MADE BY BEATING EGG WHITES UNTIL FROTHY AND STIFF. ADD 1 TABLESPOON SUGAR FOR EACH EGG WHITE, BEATING WELL AFTER EACH ADDITION. THE WHITES SHOULD BE STIFF AND HOLD UP IN PEAKS.
17. SPREAD MERINGUE OVER TOP OF MOCHA JELLY.
18. BAKE 12 TO 15 MINUTES AT 300° F. ON THIRD SHELF OF YOUR OVEN.

WOULD YOU BELIEVE THIS IS A TRULY SIMPLE PIE TO MAKE? THE MANY STEPS IN METHOD ARE GIVEN TO REMOVE ALL GUESSWORK IN PREPARING THE TWO FILLINGS WHICH COMPRISE THIS UNUSUAL FLAVORED PIE.

✛

181.

SCOTCH PIE

1½ QUARTS DICED APPLES, TART PIE APPLES PREFERRED.
½ CUP WHITE SUGAR
1 CUP BROWN SUGAR
¾ CUP FLOUR
½ CUP BUTTER
½ CUP CHOPPED PECANS

1. BUTTER A PIE TIN FREELY.
2. FILL THE TIN WITH THE DICED APPLES. THIS SHOULD MAKE A HEAPING MOUND.
3. SPRINKLE THE WHITE SUGAR OVER THE TOP.
4. RUB THE BROWN SUGAR AND FLOUR TOGETHER WITH THE BUTTER.
5. PACK THIS OVER THE TOP COVERING THE APPLES COMPLETELY.
6. SPRINKLE THE NUTS OVER THIS AND PRESS THEM SLIGHTLY INTO THE APPLES.
7. BAKE AT 350° F. UNTIL APPLES ARE TENDER.
8. ALLOW THE PIE TO COOL. CUT AND SERVE WITH A GENEROUS AMOUNT OF WHIPPED CREAM.

182.

SOUTHERN BLACK WALNUT PIE

5 EGGS
1½ CUPS DARK CORN SYRUP
¾ CUP SUGAR
2 TABLESPOONS BUTTER
1 TEASPOON VANILLA
1 CUP BLACK WALNUTS

1. BEAT THE EGGS SLIGHTLY.
2. ADD THE SYRUP AND MIX WELL.
3. ADD THE SUGAR, MELTED BUTTER, AND VANILLA. MIX.
4. FOLD IN 1 CUP OF BLACK WALNUTS, CUT IN HALF OR HALVES OF PECANS. DO NOT CHOP NUTS.
5. POUR INTO AN UNBAKED PIE SHELL. BAKE AT 400° F. FOR 10 MINUTES. REDUCE HEAT TO 350° F. AND CONTINUE BAKING FOR 50 MINUTES LONGER.
6. ALLOW PIE TO COOL AND SERVE WITH WHIPPED CREAM. THIS MAKES ONE 8 INCH PIE. SERVES 8 TO 10 GUESTS.

SOUTHERN PECAN PIE IS MADE BY THIS RECIPE USING PECANS IN PLACE OF BLACK WALNUTS.

SOUTHERN PLUM DUM PIE

3 EGG YOLKS
I CUP SUGAR
5 TABLESPOONS CREAM
I TABLESPOON BUTTER
I TEASPOON VANILLA
½ CUP TART PLUM JELLY

1. BEAT EGGS, ADD SUGAR, CREAM, MELTED BUTTER, AND VANILLA.
2. BAKE IN A RAW PIE SHELL UNTIL SET AT 350° F. FOR 40 MINUTES.
3. REMOVE FROM OVEN AND DOT OVER THE TOP WITH PLUM JELLY. COVER THIS WITH A MERINGUE AND BAKE SLOWLY FOR 15 MINUTES AT 300° F.

MERINGUE

4 EGG WHITES
½ CUP SUGAR

1. BEAT EGG WHITES UNTIL FROTHY, ADD SUGAR AND BEAT UNTIL THE EGG WHITES HOLD THEIR FORM IN SHARP PEAKS.
2. SPREAD OVER TOP OF PIE. BAKE 15 MINUTES AT 300° F.

184.

TOASTED BRAZIL NUT PIE

I BAKED PIE SHELL
5 TABLESPOONS FLOUR
¾ CUP SUGAR
2 CUPS MILK
3 EGGS
¼ TEASPOON SALT
1½ TEASPOONS VANILLA
I CUP SHAVED BRAZIL NUTS

1. SCALD MILK IN A DOUBLE BOILER.
2. MIX FLOUR WITH THE SUGAR.
3. ADD TO THE SCALDED MILK STIRRING IN ORDER TO PRE-VENT LUMPING.
4. STIR FREQUENTLY AND COOK FOR 12 MINUTES.
5. ADD EGG YOLKS BEATEN UNTIL LIGHT. REDUCE THE HEAT BELOW THE DOUBLE BOILER DURING THIS PRO-CESS.
6. COOK 3 MINUTES. ADD VANILLA AND SALT.
7. ALLOW TO COOL UNTIL TEPID.
8. FILL THE BAKED PIE SHELL.
9. BEAT EGG WHITES UNTIL FROTHY AND STIFF. ADD I TABLESPOON OF SUGAR FOR EACH EGG WHITE, BEAT-ING WELL AFTER EACH ADDITION. THE WHITES SHOULD BE STIFF AND HOLD UP IN PEAKS.
10. SPREAD THE MERINGUE OVER THE TOP OF THE FILLING. SPRINKLE WITH SHAVED BRAZIL NUTS AND BAKE 12 TO 15 MINUTES AT 300° F. ON THIRD SHELF OF YOUR OVEN.

185.

NOTES

187.

188.

NOTES

189.

8.

POTATOES AND VEGETABLES

Ordinary methods of preparation can be "dressed up" occasionally by using a new combination. I do not believe, however, that we can improve upon simple cookery for vegetables—serve them cooked at the last moment, serve them au naturel with mild seasonings and butter. From the nutritional standpoint there can be nothing better.

191.

BEETS RUSSE

2 CUPS HOT CUBED BEETS
½ CUP FRENCH DRESSING
½ CUP MINCED FINE GREEN
ONION
1 CUP SOUR CREAM
(WHIPPED)

1. MIX HOT BEETS WITH FRENCH DRESSING.
2. PLACE IN SERVING DISH. TOP WITH WHIPPED CREAM.
SPRINKLE WITH MINCED ONION.

BRUSSEL SPROUTS WITH
ROQUEFORT RAREBIT

1 PINT OF BRUSSEL SPROUTS
2 CUPS CREAM SAUCE
2 TABLESPOONS ROQUEFORT
CHEESE

1. COOK THE SPROUTS.
2. FLAKE CHEESE INTO HOT CREAM SAUCE AND STIR TO
BLEND.
3. SERVE WITH THE SAUCE OVER THE SPROUTS.
4. THE RECIPE FOR CREAM SAUCE MAY BE FOUND ON
PAGE 194.

CAULIFLOWER BAKED WITH TOASTED ALMONDS

1 HEAD CAULIFLOWER
2 CUPS CREAM SAUCE
¾ CUP CHOPPED TOASTED ALMONDS
SALT AND PEPPER
½ CUP BUTTER

1. SEPARATE CAULIFLOWER INTO FLOWERETS. COOK FOR 10 MINUTES.
2. PLACE IN A BUTTERED BAKING DISH.
3. POUR CREAM SAUCE OVER CAULIFLOWERETS AND DOT WITH BUTTER.
4. SPRINKLE WITH CHOPPED ALMONDS.
5. COVER AND BAKE FOR 30 MINUTES AT 350° F.

❖

COCONUT CARROTS

2 CUPS GRATED CARROTS
1 CUP GRATED FRESH
   COCONUT
¾ CUP BROWN SUGAR
½ CUP WATER

1. MIX CARROTS AND COCONUT WITH SUGAR.
2. PLACE IN A BUTTERED BAKING DISH AND SPRINKLE WATER OVER CARROTS.
3. BAKE AT 350° F. FOR 30 MINUTES.

CREAM SAUCE

4 TABLESPOONS FLOUR
4 TABLESPOONS BUTTER
2 CUPS MILK
¼ TEASPOON SALT
   FEW GRAINS PEPPER

1. MELT BUTTER, ADD FLOUR. STIR WHILE COOKING 3 MINUTES.
2. ADD HOT MILK, CONTINUE STIRRING WHILE COOKING 5 MINUTES.
3. SEASON TO TASTE.

194.

FRIED RICE

1 CUP LONG GRAIN RICE
(WHITE)
¾ CUP COOKED CHICKEN,
CUT IN SMALL PIECES,
SQUARES ¼ INCH THICK
¾ CUP DICED, BAKED HAM,
CUT SAME AS CHICKEN
1/3 CUP SMALL CUT GREEN
PEPPER, ¼ INCH CUBES
½ CUP FINELY CUT ONION
1 CUP BEAN SPROUTS
1 CUP BEAN SPROUT
LIQUOR
2 CUPS CHICKEN BROTH
2 OUNCES MUSHROOMS
(CUT PIECES)
LIQUID FROM THE
CANNED MUSHROOMS
¼ CUP COOKING OIL
2 HARD BOILED EGGS,
FORCED THROUGH A
SIEVE

1. WASH RICE WELL. PLACE OIL IN COVERED SKILLET. ADD
RICE AND STIR WITH A FORK. COVER AND BROWN,
STIRRING FREQUENTLY SO AS NOT TO BURN.
2. ADD ½ CUP OF CHICKEN BROTH AND ½ CUP OF THE
BEAN LIQUID. COVER RICE AND ALLOW TO COOK AT
MEDIUM HEAT FOR 15 MINUTES.

195.

3. ADD ½ CUP OF CHICKEN BROTH AND ½ CUP OF BEAN LIQUID. COOK FOR 15 MINUTES.
4. ADD ½ CUP OF CHICKEN BROTH AND COOK 15 MINUTES.
5. ADD ½ CUP OF CHICKEN BROTH AND COOK 15 MINUTES.
6. AT THIS POINT ABOUT 1 HOUR AND 15 MINUTES OF COOKING THE RICE SHOULD BE TENDER AND PRACTICALLY COOKED. ADD THE ONIONS AND COVER FOR FIVE MINUTES.
7. ADD HAM, CHICKEN, BEAN SPROUTS, MUSHROOMS AND GREEN PEPPER. COOK FIVE MINUTES MORE, TURNING THE RICE CAREFULLY IN ORDER TO HAVE ALL THOROUGHLY HEATED. DO NOT BREAK THE RICE KERNELS.
8. SALT AND PEPPER A BIT IF YOU LIKE. THEN ADD EGGS.

THIS DELECTABLE RICE DISH IS ALWAYS WELCOME.

196.

ORANGE BEETS

1 CAN FROZEN ORANGE JUICE
1 CAN WATER, USE ORANGE JUICE CAN TO MEASURE
¾ CUP CIDER VINEGAR
1¼ CUPS BROWN SUGAR
2 TABLESPOONS CORN-STARCH
1 TABLESPOON BUTTER
1 NO. 2½ CAN OF BEETS, WHOLE SMALL TYPE

1. MOISTEN THE CORNSTARCH AND SMOOTH TO A PASTE USING ½ OF THE WATER.
2. MIX ALL THE OTHER INGREDIENTS WITH THE EXCEPTION OF THE BUTTER AND BEETS.
3. BRING TO A BOIL AND ADD THE CORNSTARCH. STIR TO PREVENT LUMPING AND COOK UNTIL CLEAR AND THICK-ENED, APPROXIMATELY 8 MINUTES.
4. ADD THE BUTTER, THEN THE BEETS. HEAT WELL AND SERVE.

THIS METHOD OF PREPARING BEETS IS VERY POPULAR WITH OUR BOONE TAVERN GUESTS.

197.

RAISIN FILLED SWEET POTATOES

1 EGG YOLK
4 CUPS MASHED SWEET
POTATOES
1 TEASPOON SALT
1/8 TEASPOON CINNAMON
1/8 TEASPOON GINGER
1/8 CUP MELTED BUTTER

1. BEAT EGG SLIGHTLY. ADD MASHED POTATOES, THEN SEASONINGS AND BLEND TOGETHER. ADD MELTED BUTTER.
2. SHAPE INTO NESTS ON A GREASED BAKING SHEET USING A PASTRY BAG OR SPOON.
3. BAKE AT 450° F. UNTIL EDGES ARE SLIGHTLY BROWNED OR APPROXIMATELY 20 MINUTES.
4. FILL CENTERS WITH:

1 CUP ORANGE JUICE
1/2 CUP SUGAR
1 TABLESPOON CORN-
STARCH
1 TABLESPOON FINELY
SLICED ORANGE PEEL
1 CUP SEEDLESS RAISINS

1. BLEND ORANGE JUICE WITH SUGAR AND CORNSTARCH.
2. COOK OVER LOW HEAT STIRRING UNTIL MIXTURE THICKENS.
3. ADD ORANGE PEEL AND RAISINS. COOK 3 MINUTES. SERVE IN THE POTATO CASES.

SPINACH SUPREME

1½ LB. SPINACH
3 TABLESPOONS BUTTER
2 EGG YOLKS
4 TABLESPOONS CREAM
SALT
PEPPER
PAPRIKA

1. WASH SPINACH, COOK IN COVERED KETTLE WITHOUT WATER FOR 5 MINUTES. IF FROZEN SPINACH IS USED, 1 LB. WILL BE ENOUGH.
2. CHOP AFTER COOKING. PUT INTO SAUCE PAN WITH BUTTER. STIR AND COOK 5 MINUTES. ADD EGG YOLK MIXED WITH CREAM. SEASON WITH SALT, PEPPER AND PAPRIKA. COOK 1 MINUTE.

SERVE IN A MOUND SURROUNDED BY COOKED NOODLES.

SOUTHERN HOMINY PUDDING

1 PINT MILK, SCALDED
3 EGGS, BEATEN WELL
3 CUPS CANNED YELLOW
HOMINY

1. GRIND HOMINY USING A MEDIUM COARSE GRINDER.
2. BEAT EGGS AND ADD MILK.
3. ADD HOMINY.
4. POUR INTO WELL BUTTERED CASSEROLE AND BAKE AT 350° F. UNTIL FIRM, APPROXIMATELY 40 MINUTES.

SOUTHERN CORN PUDDING

USE THE SAME RECIPE AS FOR HOMINY PUDDING SUBSTITUTING WHOLE KERNEL YELLOW CORN FOR THE HOMINY. IN STEP 2 OF THE METHOD ADD THE FOLLOWING INGREDIENTS:

3 TABLESPOONS SIFTED FLOUR
2 TEASPOONS SALT
1 TABLESPOON SUGAR
1 TABLESPOON MELTED
BUTTER

BEAT THE EGGS AND ADD THESE INGREDIENTS MIXING WELL. NEXT ADD THE MILK AND GROUND CORN MIXING WELL.

200.

SWEET POTATO AND APPLE BAKE

3 MEDIUM SIZED SWEET
POTATOES
1 CUP BROWN SUGAR
1/2 TEASPOON SALT
3 MEDIUM SIZED COOKING
APPLES, TART
1 CUP APPLE JUICE
1/4 CUP BUTTER

1. BOIL THE POTATOES, EITHER PEELED OR UNPEELED. COOKING TIME 15 MINUTES. THE POTATOES NEED NOT BE COMPLETELY COOKED UNTIL SOFT AS IT WILL COOK IN THE OVEN LATER.
2. PEEL AND SLICE THE APPLES.
3. PEEL AND SLICE THE POTATOES, ABOUT 1/4 INCH THICK.
4. PUT THE POTATOES AND APPLES ALTERNATELY IN A BUTTERED BAKING DISH. HAVE EACH SLICE OVERLAP THE NEXT.
5. DOT WITH BUTTER AND SPRINKLE WITH 1/3 OF THE SUGAR AND 1/4 TEASPOON SALT. REPEAT YOUR LAYERS. POUR APPLE JUICE OVER LAYERS.
6. COVER AND PLACE IN A 350° F. OVEN FOR 1/2 HOUR. REMOVE THE COVER AND SPRINKLE TOP WITH THE REMAINING 1/3 SUGAR. ALLOW TO BAKE 20 TO 30 MINUTES LONGER TO MELT SUGAR AND BROWN TOP SLIGHTLY.

THIS RECIPE WILL SERVE 6 TO 8 GUESTS.

SWEET POTATO CIDER

6 BOILED SWEET POTATOES
1½ CUP BROWN SUGAR
¼ TEASPOON SALT
¼ CUP BUTTER
I CUP APPLE CIDER

1. BOIL SUGAR AND CIDER 10 MINUTES. ADD BUTTER AND SALT.
2. CUT BOILED POTATOES IN HALF. PLACE IN A BUTTERED BAKING DISH.
3. POUR COOKED SYRUP OVER POTATOES. BAKE ONE HOUR AT 350° F. BASTING FREQUENTLY WITH THE SYRUP.

SWEET POTATO COCONUT

4 BOILED SWEET POTATOES
I CUP BROWN SUGAR
¼ CUP BUTTER
I CUP FRESH COARSELY GRATED COCONUT

1. CUT POTATOES IN HALF AND PLACE IN BAKING DISH. DOT WITH BUTTER AND SPRINKLE WITH BROWN SUGAR.
2. BAKE AT 300° F. FOR 45 MINUTES. REMOVE FROM OVEN AND SPRINKLE WITH COCONUT. RETURN TO OVEN AND BROIL COCONUT UNTIL LIGHT BROWN.

202.

SWEET POTATO PUDDING

4 MEDIUM SIZED BAKED OR
  BOILED SWEET POTATOES
3 EGGS
1 CUP BROWN SUGAR
3 TABLESPOONS OF BUTTER
1/2 PINT MILK
1/2 TEASPOON BLACK PEPPER
1/8 TEASPOON SALT

1. PEEL THE POTATOES AND RUB THEM THROUGH A SIEVE.
2. ADD THE YOLKS OF EGGS. MIX WELL.
3. ADD SUGAR, BUTTER, MILK AND LAST ADD EGG WHITES BEATEN TO A FROTH.
4. SEASON WITH SALT AND PEPPER.
5. STIR ALL THE INGREDIENTS TOGETHER THOROUGHLY UNTIL VERY SMOOTH. IT SHOULD BE LIGHT AND ALMOST LIQUID.
6. POUR INTO BUTTERED CUSTARD CUPS. PLACE IN A PAN OF HOT WATER. BAKE AT 350° F. FOR ONE HOUR UNTIL WELL BROWN.

THIS MAKES 10 SERVINGS.

203.

SWEET POTATO ROYALE

4 SMOOTH MEDIUM SIZED
SWEET POTATOES
1/2 CUP CHOPPED NUTS
1/2 CUP FINE CUT PINEAPPLE
(CANNED)
1/2 CUP CUT MARASCHINO
CHERRIES
3 EGG WHITES
3 TABLESPOONS SUGAR

1. WASH, DRY AND GREASE THE POTATOES WITH BUTTER SUBSTITUTE. PLACE IN A PAN TO BAKE AT 450° F. FOR 40 MINUTES OR UNTIL SOFT WHEN TRIED WITH A FORK. REMOVE FROM THE OVEN AND CUT IN HALF LENGTHWISE. REMOVE THE INSIDE AND MASH, ADDING ABOUT A TABLESPOON OF BUTTER AND 2 TABLESPOONS OF MILK. BEAT WELL.
2. MIX INTO THE MASHED POTATOES, THE NUTS, CHERRIES, AND PINEAPPLE. REFILL THE 8 HALF SHELLS WITH THIS MIXTURE.
3. BEAT THE EGG WHITES UNTIL THEY HOLD THEMSELVES IN PEAKS. ADD THE SUGAR AND CONTINUE BEATING TO FORM A MERINGUE. PLACE SOME OF THE MERINGUE ON TOP OF EACH POTATO. BROWN AT 300° F. FOR 10 MINUTES.

204.

TOMATO RICE

¾ CUP WASHED RICE
3 CUPS TOMATO JUICE
I SMALL ONION, FINELY CUT
¼ CUP CHOPPED PIMIENTO
½ TEASPOON SALT
¼ TEASPOON PEPPER
I TABLESPOON BUTTER

1. MIX THE FIRST 6 INGREDIENTS TOGETHER.
2. POUR INTO A WELL BUTTERED CASSEROLE.
3. DOT THE TOP WITH THE BUTTER.
4. COVER AND BAKE AT 375° F. ONE HOUR STIRRING OCCA-
   SIONALLY TO INSURE EVEN COOKING.

TOMATO SURPRISE

6 SLICES OF TOMATO
I CAN DEVILED HAM
I CUP BREAD CRUMBS
2 EGG YOLKS
2 TABLESPOONS CREAM
SALT AND PEPPER

1. BEAT EGGS, ADD CREAM.
2. MIX SALT AND PEPPER WITH BREAD CRUMBS.
3. SPREAD HAM BETWEEN TWO SLICES OF TOMATO.
4. DIP TOMATO INTO EGG WASH, THEN INTO BREAD
   CRUMBS. FRY IN A SKILLET WITH PLENTY OF FAT.

TORGOR POTATOES

6 BOILED NEW POTATOES
¾ CUP PARMESAN CHEESE
½ CUP BREAD CRUMBS
SALT AND PEPPER
2 EGG YOLKS
2 TABLESPOONS CREAM

1. BEAT EGG YOLKS AND ADD CREAM.
2. MIX THE PARMESAN CHEESE AND BREAD CRUMBS TO-
GETHER, ADD A DASH OF SALT AND PEPPER.
3. DIP EACH POTATO INTO THE EGG WASH THEN THE
CRUMB MIXTURE.
4. FRY IN DEEP FAT OR IN A SKILLET WITH CONSIDERABLE
AMOUNT OF FAT TO BROWN EVENLY ON ALL SIDES.

✣

206.

208.

NOTES

209.

9.

SALADS

Let us enjoy a salad plate for lunch.
With a few simple and tasty accom-
paniments the salad meal can prove
popular. The greater the variety of
crisp greens and raw vegetables the
more tantalizing is the TOSS TO-
GETHER SALAD. Use scissors to cut
your greens.

211.

AMBROSIA SALAD

2 PEACHES
2 GREEN GAGE PLUMS
2 APRICOTS
1 CUP HALVED GREEN
GRAPES
1 CUP GRATED FRESH
COCONUT
¾ CUP FRENCH DRESSING

1. ALL FRUIT IS FRESH.
2. CUT ALL FRUIT INTO SMALL SECTIONS AS YOU WOULD AN ORANGE.
3. MIX FRUIT TOGETHER AND PILE ON THE LETTUCE LEAF.
4. SERVE WITH FRENCH DRESSING OVER THE FRUIT AND SPRINKLE GENEROUSLY WITH THE COCONUT.
THIS SALAD SERVES 6. IN GRATING THE COCONUT USE A MEDIUM GRATER.

CALAVO SUPREME

¾ CUP COTTAGE CHEESE
½ CUP CHOPPED PECANS
¼ CUP CHOPPED RIPE OLIVES
½ TEASPOON CHOPPED FINE
CHIVES

1. MIX THE ABOVE INGREDIENTS TOGETHER. FILL HALVES OF PEELED AND STONED CALAVO OR AVOCADO PEAR.
2. WRAP IN WAXED PAPER AND TWIST THE ENDS OF PAPER TIGHT TO SECURE THE TWO CALAVO HALVES TOGETHER.
3. CHILL FOR ONE HOUR OR MORE. SLICE AND SERVE ON ENDIVE GARNISHED WITH TOMATO SECTIONS. SERVE WITH FRENCH DRESSING.

THIS WILL FILL 2 OR 3 CALAVOS.

212.

CHATEAU SALAD

2 PACKAGES OF LEMON
GELATINE
1 PINT OF GINGERALE
WHIPPED CREAM DRESSING
(PAGE 239)

1. DISSOLVE THE CONTENTS OF THE GELATINE IN TWO CUPS OF BOILING WATER.
2. GREASE A PAN 8x8 INCHES WITH COOKING OIL. POUR THE GELATINE MIXTURE INTO THE PAN.
3. WHEN THE GELATINE HAS COOLED AND JUST BEFORE IT BEGINS TO THICKEN ADD THE ICE COLD GINGERALE. (THIS STEP IS VERY IMPORTANT. THE GINGERALE WILL FOAM OVER THE MIXTURE. ALLOW TO CONGEAL.)
4. CUT IN SQUARES. SERVE WITH WHIPPED CREAM DRESSING.

THIS IS A DELICIOUS DINNER SALAD. SERVES 8 TO 10.

✣

CHICKEN SALAD BOMBAY

I CUP COOKED CUBED
CHICKEN
I CUP COOKED CUBED HAM
(BAKED HAM MAY BE USED)
I CUP CUT FRESH SPINACH,
CUT INTO HALF INCH
SQUARES
FRENCH DRESSING
I CUP SHREDDED FRESH
COCONUT
WHIPPED CREAM DRESSING
(PAGE 239)

1. MIX CHICKEN, HAM AND SPINACH WITH FRENCH DRESS-
   ING AND ALLOW TO STAND IN THE REFRIGERATOR I
   HOUR. USE ONLY ENOUGH FRENCH DRESSING TO
   MOISTEN THE MIXTURE.
2. PLACE THE SALAD IN A LETTUCE CUP USING A SCANT
   HALF CUP OF SALAD PER SERVING. TOP EACH WITH A
   GENEROUS AMOUNT OF WHIPPED CREAM DRESSING AND
   SPRINKLE WITH THE SHREDDED COCONUT.

THIS RECIPE WILL MAKE SIX MEDIUM SIZED SALADS OR
FOUR VERY LARGE SALADS. IF DESIRED TO USE AS A
MAIN COURSE I WOULD SUGGEST GARNISHING EACH
SALAD WITH TOMATO WEDGES OR CELERY HEARTS AND
A SPICED PEACH. THE SERVING OF SMALL SANDWICHES
OR A CHEESE TOAST WOULD BE A NICE ACCOMPANI-
MENT.

CHICKEN SALAD INDIA

1½ CUPS CUBED COOKED
CHICKEN, ¼" CUBES
½ CUP CUBED BAKED HAM,
¼" CUBES
¾ CUP COLD FLAKY RICE
½ CUP FINELY CHOPPED
CHUTNEY
1 CUP SHREDDED FRESH
COCONUT
WHIPPED CREAM
DRESSING
(PAGE 239)
4 LETTUCE LEAF CUPS

1. MIX THE CHICKEN, HAM, RICE, AND CHUTNEY TO-
GETHER.
2. PLACE THE LETTUCE CUPS ON SALAD PLATE AND FILL
WITH THE SALAD.
3. SHOWER THE TOPS OF EACH SALAD GENEROUSLY WITH
THE SHREDDED COCONUT.
4. SERVE WHIPPED CREAM DRESSING.
THIS RECIPE SERVES 4.

YOU MAY WISH TO ADD TOMATO WEDGES, FRESH PINE-
APPLE WEDGES, LEMON SLICES, AND POTATO CHIPS TO
COMPLETE THIS LUNCH SALAD. HOT ROLLS OR AS-
SORTED BREADS WOULD BE A FINE ACCOMPANIMENT.

CHICKEN SALAD TROPICALE

1 CUP CUBED CHICKEN (COOKED)
½ CUP CUT CELERY
SALT AND PEPPER
1 CUP WHIPPED CREAM DRESSING (PAGE 239)
1 CALAVO OR AVOCADO PEAR
1 LEMON
2 MELBA PEACH HALVES
½ CUP SHREDDED FRESH COCONUT (COARSELY SHREDDED)
½ CUP WHIPPED CREAM

1. MIX CHICKEN, CELERY, SALT AND PEPPER WITH ¾ CUP OF THE WHIPPED CREAM DRESSING.
2. PLACE A PEACH HALF ON A LETTUCE LEAF. FILL THE CENTER WITH CHICKEN SALAD.
3. MASH THE RIPE CALAVO AND ADD THE JUICE OF THE LEMON. NEXT MIX WITH ½ CUP WHIPPED CREAM.
4. SPREAD THE CALAVO MIXTURE OVER THE TOPS OF THE CHICKEN SALAD. SPRINKLE WITH THE FRESH COCONUT.
5. IF YOU PREFER, THE COCONUT MAY BE TOASTED IN THE GRILL A FEW MINUTES BEFORE COVERING THE TOP OF THE SALAD.

THIS SALAD COULD BE ACCOMPANIED WITH NUT BREAD AND BUTTER SANDWICHES OR AN ASSORTMENT OF BREADS AND ROLLS.

216.

CHICKEN AND VEGETABLE SALAD
IN TOMATO ROSETTE

1½ CUPS CUBED COOKED
    CHICKEN
¼ CUP COOKED FRESH PEAS
¼ CUP COOKED SMALL
    CARROT CUBES
½ CUP FINELY CUT CELERY
1 CUP WHIPPED CREAM
½ CUP MAYONNAISE
    SALT AND PEPPER
1 TEASPOON LEMON JUICE
4 TOMATOES, MEDIUM SIZE
    LETTUCE LEAVES

1. MIX CHICKEN, VEGETABLES, CELERY, WHIPPED CREAM AND MAYONNAISE TOGETHER. STIR IN THE LEMON JUICE AND SEASON THE SALAD.
2. CUT STEM PART OUT OF TOP OF THE TOMATO AND THEN BY CUTTING EACH TOMATO THROUGH ALMOST TO THE BASE MAKE FOUR CUTS WHICH WILL GIVE YOU EIGHT SECTIONS. WITH YOUR FINGERS SPREAD THESE PETALS TO FORM A ROSETTE CUP. PLACE CUP ON A LETTUCE LEAF AND FILL WITH SALAD MIXTURE. THIS MAKES 4 SALADS.

TOASTED ENGLISH MUFFINS AND JAM WITH THIS COMBINATION SEEMS MOST SATISFACTORY. YOU MAY TOAST HALVES OF LARGE BAKING POWDER BISCUITS IF ENGLISH MUFFINS ARE NOT AVAILABLE.

COOL MELON SALAD

2 PACKAGES OF STRAW-
BERRY GELATINE
2 CUPS OF FRESH BLUE-
BERRIES
4 CUPS OF FRESH WATER-
MELON AND HONEY DEW
MELON BALLS

1. PREPARE THE GELATINE AS DIRECTED ON THE PACKAGE MAKING TWO PINTS.
2. OIL A SQUARE PAN WITH COOKING OIL TO FACILITATE REMOVING SALAD. COVER THE BOTTOM OF THE PAN WITH MELON BALLS. IF ONLY WATERMELON IS AVAILABLE THAT MAY BE USED ENTIRELY.
3. POUR THE SLIGHTLY THICKENED AND COOLED GELATINE OVER THE MELON BALLS.
4. SPRINKLE BLUEBERRIES ON TOP.
5. PLACE IN REFRIGERATOR TO SET.
6. WHEN CONGEALED CUT INTO SQUARES. SERVE WITH 1 CUP WHIPPED CREAM MIXED WITH 1/2 CUP OF MAYONNAISE.

THIS IS A REFRESHING DINNER SALAD ON A SUMMER DAY. SERVES 8 TO 10.

FRESH PEAR SALAD

3 PEARS
1 CUP FINELY DICED CELERY
1/2 CUP CHOPPED NUTS
1 CUP WHIPPED CREAM
1/2 CUP MAYONNAISE

1. CUT THE PEAR INTO SMALL DICED PIECES.
2. ADD THE DICED CELERY AND MIX WELL.
3. FOLD MAYONNAISE INTO STIFFLY BEATEN WHIPPED CREAM. ADD TO SALAD MIXTURE.
4. SERVE ON A LETTUCE LEAF TOPPED WITH A BIT OF CREAM DRESSING. SPRINKLE WITH CHOPPED NUTS.

THIS WILL MAKE 6 SALADS.

✣

FRESH SHRIMPS ON SHREDDED LETTUCE

12 JUMBO SHRIMPS
2 HARD COOKED EGGS
COCKTAIL SAUCE
LETTUCE

1. REMOVE THE VISCERA FROM SHRIMP AND PLACE THEM ON ICE TO CHILL.
2. SLICE EGGS WITH EGG SLICER.
3. ARRANGE LETTUCE LEAVES ON TWO PLATES. IN THE CENTER PLACE A FEW SHREDS OF CUT LETTUCE TO FORM A BED.
4. LAY SHRIMP IN A ROW LENGTHWISE ON LETTUCE BED.
5. ON EACH SIDE OF SHRIMPS LAY SLICES OF EGG. YOU WILL USE SIX SHRIMPS FOR EACH PLATE.
6. SERVE COCKTAIL SAUCE WITH THE SALAD. SOME GUESTS PREFER A SERVING OF FRENCH DRESSING TO GO WITH THE LETTUCE. THE RECIPE FOR COCKTAIL SAUCE IS FOUND ON PAGE 109.

FOR LUNCH TRY SERVING A HOT SOUP, THIS SALAD ALONG WITH HOT BUTTERED RYE TOAST, BEVERAGE AND A RICH DESSERT.

FROZEN STUFFED BELL PEPPER SALAD

1 CUP COTTAGE CHEESE
1/3 CUP ROQUEFORT CHEESE
5 MEDIUM PEPPERS (TO BE STUFFED)
1/4 CUP RADISH, CHOPPED FINE
1/4 CUP CHIVES, CHOPPED FINE
1/3 CUP MAYONNAISE
1/4 CUP RAW CAULIFLOWER, CHOPPED FINE

1. MIX ALL THE INGREDIENTS TOGETHER EXCEPT THE MAYONNAISE. WHEN OTHER INGREDIENTS ARE WELL BLENDED ADD MAYONNAISE.
2. WASH AND REMOVE THE SEEDS FROM THE GREEN PEPPERS.
3. FILL THE PEPPERS WITH THE MIXTURE AND PLACE IN THE FREEZING UNIT OF YOUR REFRIGERATOR. TWO HOURS OUGHT TO BE SUFFICIENT FOR THE FREEZING OF THE PEPPERS.
4. SLICE EACH PEPPER INTO ROUNDS ABOUT 1/4 INCH THICK. SERVE THREE OR FOUR SLICES ON A LETTUCE LEAF DEPENDING ON THE SIZE OF THE SALAD YOU DESIRE.
5. SERVE WITH FRENCH DRESSING.

SHOULD THE PEPPER CRUMBLE IN THE SLICING PROCESS YOU MAY FIND IT NECESSARY TO REASSEMBLE THE PIECES ON THE PLATE. A VERY SHARP KNIFE IS NEEDED TO CUT THROUGH THE PEPPER.

221.

FRESH FRUIT IMPERIAL

ORANGES	GRAPEFRUIT	CANTALOUPE
GRAPES	PEARS	BLACKBERRIES
WATERMELON	STRAWBERRIES	PLUMS (RED AND
BLUEBERRIES	DATES	GREEN)
PEACHES	NECTARINES	APPLES
PINEAPPLE	NUTS	RAISINS
COTTAGE CHEESE	BANANAS	

1. PURCHASE AS MANY OF THE FRUITS AS YOU FIND AVAIL-ABLE AT THE MARKET. BUY AN AMOUNT YOU WOULD REQUIRE FOR THE NUMBER OF SALADS YOU DESIRE TO MAKE.

2. CUT THE FOLLOWING FRUITS IN SECTIONS APPROXI-MATELY THE SAME SIZE: ORANGES, GRAPEFRUIT, APPLES, PEARS, PEACHES, NECTARINES, AND PLUMS. I SUGGEST YOU PEEL ONLY THE ORANGES, GRAPEFRUIT AND PEACHES.

3. PEEL THE PINEAPPLE, CUT IN SLICES $\frac{1}{2}$ INCH THICK, THEN CUT IN HALF AND CUT EACH SLICE IN WEDGE SHAPED PIECES.

4. PEEL THE CANTALOUPE AND CUT IN LONG SECTION SHAPED PIECES. THE WATERMELON IS SCOOPED OUT WITH A BALL CUTTING SPOON.

5. SLICE THE BANANA IN HALF LENGTHWISE THEN CUT IN HALF AND CUT EACH HALF LENGTHWISE.

6. THE BERRIES, DATES, AND NUTS ARE LEFT WHOLE.

7. BEGIN YOUR FRUIT MOUND BY PLACING A LARGE LET-TUCE LEAF UPON A PLATE. BY ADDING ANOTHER LET-TUCE LEAF OPPOSITE THE FIRST AND ALLOWING THE LEAVES TO INTERLAP YOU WILL HAVE A BASKET OR CUP

222.

SHAPE ON THE PLATE. IN THIS CUP PLACE A SMALL AMOUNT OF SHREDDED LETTUCE.

8. NOW ADD THE FRUITS IN ALTERNATE FASHION FORMING A CIRCLE:

CANTALOUPE, GRAPEFRUIT, BANANAS, ORANGE, APPLE, PEACH, PINEAPPLE, PLUM, PEAR, NECTARINE AND REPEAT; CONTINUE EACH CIRCLE OF FRUIT PILED ON TOP OF THE OTHER. EACH ROW INDENTED ON THE FORMER ROW SO THAT IN TIME YOU WILL HAVE A COMPLETED MOUND OR PYRAMID WHICH FLARES OUT FROM THE TOP TO ITS BOTTOM AND OUTSIDE EDGE. THE DATES, BERRIES, NUTS AND WATERMELON BALLS ARE USED THROUGHOUT THE CIRCULAR ARRANGEMENT ADDING THEM INTO THE DESIGN AS YOU BUILD UP THE MOUND. ON THE TOP PLACE A BALL OF COTTAGE CHEESE AND SHOWER A GENEROUS AMOUNT OF CHOPPED NUTS AND RAISINS OVER THE CHEESE. SERVE WITH FRENCH DRESSING. PLACE A SMALL CLUSTER OF GRAPES ON THE STEM AT THE SIDE AND BASE OF THE FRUIT MOUND.

THIS SALAD IS QUITE THE MOST EYE APPEALING AND TASTE SATISFYING OF ALL THE LARGE FRUIT SALADS. ONE NEEDS NO MORE THAN SOME CINNAMON TOAST AND BEVERAGE TO COMPLETE A DELIGHTFUL LUNCH OR SUPPER. LET YOUR APPETITE BE YOUR GUIDE IN JUST HOW GRAND AND LARGE THE SALAD WILL BE.

223.

GREEN BAY SALAD

2 PACKAGES LEMON
GELATINE DESSERT POWDER
3 CUPS FINELY CUT CELERY
1 CUP COARSELY CUT
ALMONDS
1 CUP FINELY CUT STUFFED
OLIVES
WHIPPED CREAM DRESSING

1. PREPARE GELATINE AS DIRECTED ON THE PACKAGE.
2. OIL A PAN WITH SALAD OIL AND COVER THE BOTTOM
AND EVENLY DISTRIBUTE MIXED CELERY, OLIVES AND
NUTS.
3. POUR THE SLIGHTLY THICKENED GELATINE OVER THE
MIXTURE.
4. WHEN CONGEALED CUT AND SERVE ON LETTUCE LEAVES.

THIS WILL SERVE 16 GUESTS. FOR THE REQUIRED
AMOUNT OF WHIPPED CREAM DRESSING USE THE REC-
IPE ON PAGE 239. YOU WILL FIND THIS DINNER SALAD
IS VERY TASTY WHEN SERVED WITH CREAMED CHICKEN
DISHES AND ALMOST ALL TYPES OF MEATS. THIS IS A
FAVORITE FOR BUFFET SUPPERS AND GOES ESPECIALLY
WELL WITH BAKED HAM.

HAM AND ROQUEFORT ROLL

I CUP COTTAGE CHEESE
3 TABLESPOONS FLAKED
ROQUEFORT CHEESE
I TABLESPOON CHOPPED
CHIVES
CREAM, IF NEEDED
4 THIN SLICES BAKED HAM
4 SMALL LETTUCE LEAVES
FILLED WITH POTATO
SALAD

1. MIX COTTAGE CHEESE WITH THE ROQUEFORT CHEESE
   AND CHIVES. ADD A BIT OF CREAM IF NEEDED TO MAKE
   A SOFT MIXTURE.
2. SPREAD THE HAM WITH THE MIXTURE AND MAKE INTO
   A ROLL. PLACE ON PLATE WITH THE LAPPING PIECE OF
   HAM ROLL DOWNWARD ON THE PLATE. SERVE WITH
   A SMALL SERVING OF POTATO SALAD.

THIS WILL MAKE 4 ROLLS. SERVE WITH THIN CRACKERS
OR SIMILAR WAFER.

225.

KADOTA FIG AND PEACH CIRCLE WITH ALMOND CREAM

4 KADOTA FIGS
1/2 CUP PEANUT BUTTER
CREAMED TOGETHER WITH
2 TABLESPOONS H O N E Y
AND 1/4 CUP CHOPPED
NUTS
1/2 CUP WHIPPED CREAM
MIXED WITH 1/4 CUP SIFTED
CONFECTIONERS SUGAR
AND 1/4 TEASPOON OF
ALMOND EXTRACT
4 HALVES MELBA PEACHES

1. FILL FIGS WITH THE CREAMED PEANUT BUTTER MIXTURE. EACH FIG SHOULD BE STUFFED FULL AND POPPING OPEN.
2. PLACE A FIG IN THE CENTER OF EACH MELBA PEACH.
3. SERVE TWO FILLED PEACH HALVES ON A LETTUCE LEAF.
4. GARNISH THROUGH THE CENTER OF EACH PEACH WITH A PORTION OF THE WHIPPED MIXTURE.

THIS MAKES 2 SALAD PLATES.

THIS IS A FRUIT PLATE LUNCH AND WOULD BE TASTY WITH TOASTED CHEESE SANDWICHES USING THE RECIPE FOR SNAPPY CHEESE SPREAD FOUND ON PAGE 20.

226.

LOBSTER SALAD JAPANESE

1 CUP FRESH OR CANNED
LOBSTER MEAT
½ CUP BAMBOO SHOOTS
½ CUP WATER CHESTNUTS,
CUT IN THIN SLICES
¼ CUP PISTACHIO NUTS
1 TEASPOON LEMON JUICE
SALT AND PEPPER
¼ CUP CHOPPED ALMONDS
1 CUP WHIPPED CREAM
½ CUP MAYONNAISE

1. MIX THE LOBSTER FLAKES, BAMBOO SHOOTS, WATER
   CHESTNUTS, ALMONDS, LEMON JUICE, SALT AND PEPPER
2. LINE A SALAD BOWL, INDIVIDUAL SIZE, WITH A LETTUCE
   LEAF. ADD A BIT OF SHREDDED LETTUCE AS A BASE.
   PLACE SALAD IN THE BOWL AND TOP WITH THE WHIPPED
   CREAM MIXED WITH THE MAYONNAISE.
3. SPRINKLE WITH PISTACHIO NUTS.

THIS WILL MAKE TWO SALAD BOWLS.

227.

MOLDED BLACK CHERRY SALAD

2 PACKAGES GELATINE DESSERT POWDER, CHERRY FLAVOR
2 CUPS PITTED BLACK CHERRIES, CANNED
½ CUP CHOPPED NUTS
1½ CUPS FINELY CUT CELERY

1. PREPARE GELATINE AS DIRECTED ON THE PACKAGE.
2. OIL INDIVIDUAL MOLDS OR A SQUARE PAN WITH SALAD OIL TO FACILITATE REMOVING SALAD FROM THE PAN.
3. COVER BOTTOM OF THE PAN WITH A MIXTURE OF CHERRIES, NUTS AND CELERY.
4. ADD THE COOLED AND SLIGHTLY THICKENED GELATINE.
5. SERVE WITH WHIPPED CREAM DRESSING (PAGE 239).

THIS WILL MAKE 16 SALADS.

✣

PINEAPPLE AND BARTLETT PEAR CIRCLE, SEAFOAM TOAST

4 PINEAPPLE RINGS
1 CUP CREAM CHEESE
4 BARTLETT PEAR HALVES
½ TEASPOON BAKING POWDER

1. PLACE A PEAR ON A LETTUCE LEAF.
2. PLACE HALF A RING OF PINEAPPLE ON EACH SIDE OF THE PEAR.
3. MIX CREAM CHEESE WITH BAKING POWDER. SPREAD ON 4 PIECES OF TOASTED WHOLE WHEAT OR WHITE BREAD. PLACE UNDER THE GRILL. WHEN LIGHTLY BROWNED RE-MOVE AND CUT INTO 4 TRIANGLES. SERVE AROUND THE PINEAPPLE RING.

THIS SALAD MAY BE USED AS A LIGHT LUNCH.

PINEAPPLE SANDWICH SALAD, TOMATO WEDGES AND BACON STRIPS

6 SLICES CANNED PINEAPPLE
1/2 POUND COTTAGE CHEESE MIXED WITH 1/2 CUP OF WHIPPED CREAM.
1 GRAPEFRUIT
2 TOMATOES
6 SLICES BACON
1/2 AVOCADO PEAR

1. PLACE A SLICE OF PINEAPPLE ON A LETTUCE LEAF.
2. TOP PINEAPPLE SLICE WITH A SPOONFUL OF COTTAGE CHEESE MIXED WITH WHIPPED CREAM. PLACE A SECOND SLICE OF PINEAPPLE ON TOP. THIS FORMS THE SAND-WICH.
3. CUT TOMATO IN SECTIONS AS YOU WOULD AN ORANGE. PLACE A SECTION OF TOMATO, A SLICE OF AVOCADO PEAR, A SECTION OF GRAPEFRUIT AND REPEAT AROUND THE PINEAPPLE RING.
4. PLACE TWO STRIPS OF BACON ON TOP, ONE SLICE CROSSING THE OTHER. (COOK THE BACON THE LAST MINUTE IN ORDER TO SERVE IT CRISP AND HOT.)
5. SERVE WITH FRENCH DRESSING.

THIS WILL MAKE 3 SALAD PLATES. ONE MAY SERVE TOAST, HOT ROLLS, POTATO CHIPS OR OPEN FACED SANDWICHES WITH THIS SALAD TO COMPLETE A LUNCH-EON PLATE.

230.

SALAD OF FIVE FRUITS

4 BARTLETT PEARS
4 MELBA PEACHES
4 BLUE PLUMS
2 BANANAS
4 WHOLE APRICOTS
WHIPPED CREAM DRESSING
(PAGE 239)
8 LETTUCE LEAVES

1. PLACE LETTUCE LEAVES ON A SALAD PLATE ONE LEAF
   INTERLAPPING ANOTHER TO FORM A CUP SHAPE.
2. PLACE THE FRUIT ON THE LETTUCE LEAF IN A CIRCLE IN
   THE ORDER IN WHICH THEY ARE WRITTEN ABOVE. IN
   THIS WAY THE WHOLE APRICOT WILL BE NEXT TO THE
   PEAR. THE BANANA IS PEELED AND SPLIT IN HALF
   LENGTHWISE, THEN CUT IN HALF. USE A HALF OF A
   BANANA TO EACH SALAD.
3. SERVE WITH WHIPPED CREAM DRESSING.

   TOASTED CHEESE TRIANGLES ARE PARTICULARLY GOOD
   WITH THIS SALAD PLATE. TOAST A SLICE OF BREAD THEN
   SPREAD WITH SNAPPY CHEESE SPREAD AND BROIL TO
   MELT THE CHEESE. CUT THE SLICE FROM CORNER TO
   CORNER FORMING 4 TRIANGLES. THESE YOU PLACE
   AROUND THE RIM OF YOUR PLATE WITH THE POINTS OF
   THE TRIANGLES TOWARD THE OUTER RIM OF THE PLATE.
   IF THE SALAD COVERS MUCH OF THE PLATE THE TOAST
   MAY BE PLACED ON THE FRUIT AT VARIOUS ANGLES TO
   MAKE AN ATTRACTIVE LOOKING SALAD.

SAN REO CHICKEN SALAD

1 CUP CUBED DARK MEAT OF CHICKEN
1/2 CUP CUT BLACK OLIVES
1/2 CUP FINELY CUT CELERY
1 TEASPOON LEMON JUICE
SALT AND PEPPER
1/2 CUP WHIPPED CREAM
1/4 CUP MAYONNAISE
1/2 CUP SLICED BRAZIL NUTS

1. MIX CHICKEN, OLIVES, CELERY AND LEMON JUICE. ADD SALT AND PEPPER TO TASTE.
2. MIX WHIPPED CREAM AND MAYONNAISE. ADD HALF TO THE SALAD AND BLEND TOGETHER.
3. PLACE A LETTUCE LEAF ON A PLATE AND FILL WITH THE SALAD. TOP WITH MORE CREAM DRESSING AND SHOWER WITH BRAZIL NUTS.
4. THIS WILL MAKE TWO SALADS.

ORANGE MUFFINS AND SPICED FRUIT WOULD BE AN ENJOYABLE ACCOMPANIMENT TO THIS SALAD.

✤

232.

SPINACH SALAD

2 CUPS CUT RAW SPINACH
1/4 CUP CHOPPED COOKED BACON
1/4 CUP MINCED GREEN ONIONS
1 CUP SMALL CUT PIECES OF TOMATO
1/4 CUP FINELY CUT GREEN PEPPER
1/2 CUP SALAD OIL
1/4 CUP CIDER VINEGAR
SALT AND PEPPER

1. MIX ALL INGREDIENTS TOGETHER.
2. ADD OIL AND VINEGAR AND STIR.
3. ALLOW TO STAND IN REFRIGERATOR FOR 15 MINUTES.
4. SEASON TO TASTE.
5. SERVE ON LETTUCE LEAVES. SERVES 8.

✣

233.

STUFFED PEACH SALAD PLATE

6 HALVES OF MELBA
PEACHES
3 OUNCES CREAM CHEESE
1/2 CUP CHOPPED
MARASCHINO CHERRIES
1/2 CUP CHOPPED PECANS
I CUP WHIPPED CREAM
1/2 CUP MAYONNAISE

1. CREAM THE CHEESE WITH THE NUTS AND CHERRIES.
FILL CENTERS OF THE PEACHES WITH THIS MIXTURE.
2. PLACE A HALF PEACH ON TOP OF THE CHEESE CENTER,
THUS YOU WILL HAVE A WHOLE PEACH.
3. DILUTE A SMALL BIT OF RED FOOD COLORING WITH
WATER AND BRUSH OVER ONE CORNER OF THE PEACH
TO PRODUCE A BLUSH. STICK A CLOVE IN ONE END FOR
THE STEM. PLACE ON THE LETTUCE LEAF. SERVE WITH
WHIPPED CREAM MIXED WITH THE MAYONNAISE.
4. TO GARNISH . . . SHAPE A CARROT BY USING A SMALL
AMOUNT OF SNAPPY CHEESE SPREAD FOUND ON PAGE
20, FORMING THE SHAPE OF A CARROT IN YOUR FIN-
GERS. BRUSH THIS SLIGHTLY WITH A BIT OF PAPRIKA TO
BLUSH ONE SIDE OF THE CARROT. INSERT A PIECE OF
PARSLEY IN THE TOP FOR THE GREENS.

THIS RECIPE MAKES 3 SALAD PLATES. WHEN THIS IS
SERVED WITH FINGER SANDWICHES OR TOASTED MUF-
FINS IT MAKES A PLEASANT LUNCHEON DISH.

234.

STUFFED EGG SALAD

4 HARD COOKED EGGS
4 TABLESPOONS PREPARED
   CHEESE SPREAD (PURCHASE
   AT GROCERY)
4 TABLESPOONS OLIVE BUT-
   TER
   THOUSAND ISLAND DRESS-
   ING

1. REMOVE YOLKS FROM WHITES BY CUTTING EACH EGG
   IN HALF LENGTHWISE.
2. FILL 4 HALVES WITH CHEESE AND 4 WITH OLIVE BUTTER.
3. PRESS A HALF FILLED WITH CHEESE AND A HALF FILLED
   WITH OLIVE BUTTER TOGETHER.
4. SLICE WHOLE EGG THUS FORMED AND ARRANGE EACH
   ON A LETTUCE LEAF ON WHICH SOME SHREDDED GREENS
   HAVE BEEN PLACED.
5. TOP WITH THE SALAD DRESSING, OVER THIS SPRINKLE
   CHOPPED YOLKS.

THIS WILL MAKE 4 TO 6 DINNER SALADS. IT IS PARTICU-
LARLY GOOD WHEN SHREDDED ENDIVE GREENS ARE
PLACED ON THE LETTUCE LEAF.

235.

TOSS TOGETHER SALAD

1½ CUPS OF CUT PIECES OF TOMATO

1 CUP CUT UP SPINACH LEAVES (CUT WITH SCISSORS)

2 CUPS OF CUT PIECES OF LETTUCE, USE A VARIETY OF TYPES AS OAK LEAF, HEAD, LEAF, ETC., IF AVAILABLE

1 CUP CUT PIECES OF ENDIVE AND WATERCRESS IF AVAILABLE

½ CUP SHREDDED RAW CARROT

½ CUP SHREDDED CABBAGE

1 CUP SLICED CUCUMBER (SLICED VERY THIN)

½ CUP THINLY SLICED RADISHES

¾ CUP VERY SMALL BITS OF RAW CAULIFLOWER

½ CUP SLICED SMALL GREEN ONIONS

1 LARGE GREEN PEPPER (THINLY CUT)

1 CUP THINLY SLICED PIECES OF CELERY

1. COMBINE AND MIX ALL INGREDIENTS TOGETHER.
2. PLACE THE TOSSED SALAD TO CRISP IN YOUR REFRIGERATOR UNTIL SERVING TIME AND SERVE WITH FRENCH DRESSING.

236.

ICE CREAM DRESSING

1 QUART VANILLA ICE
CREAM
1 PINT VERY STIFFLY
WHIPPED CREAM
1/2 CUP MAYONNAISE
2 WELL BEATEN EGG YOLKS

1. BREAK THE ICE CREAM INTO SMALL PIECES WITH A FORK.
2. ADD THE MAYONNAISE TO THE WHIPPED CREAM.
3. MIX THE TWO TOGETHER AND FOLD IN THE EGG YOLKS.
4. WHIP TOGETHER WITH A SPOON TO MIX WELL.

IF YOU DO NOT PLAN TO USE IMMEDIATELY OR IF THE
MIXTURE HAS BECOME TOO MUSHY IN THE MIXING PRO-
CESS PLACE IN THE FREEZING SECTION OF YOUR REFRIG-
ERATOR TO RETURN THE MIXTURE TO A SOLID STATE. THE
DRESSING SHOULD BE SOFT YET HOLD ITS SHAPE WHEN
PLACED ON THE SALAD.

THIS DRESSING IS USED NICELY WITH A STUFFED BANANA
SALAD, SALAD OF FIVE FRUITS, OVER SLICES OF CANTA-
LOUPE AND HONEY DEW MELON, WITH ANY FRESH
FRUIT OR BERRY SALAD ARRANGEMENT.

USUALLY ALLOW APPROXIMATELY 1/2 CUP OF DRESSING
PER SALAD. THIS RECIPE MAKES 8 TO 10 SERVINGS.

FRENCH DRESSING

¾ CUP SALAD OIL
1/3 CUP CIDER VINEGAR
¾ TEASPOON SALT
½ TEASPOON PEPPER

1. PUT ALL TOGETHER IN A GLASS JAR OR DRESSING SHAKER AND SHAKE WELL.
2. SERVE THE DRESSING OVER THE SALAD AT TIME OF SERVING. YOU MAY LIKE TO ADD 4 TABLESPOONS OF CHILI SAUCE TO THE DRESSING FOR VARIETY OR CRUMBLE 1¼ OUNCES OF ROQUEFORT CHEESE INTO THE DRESSING.

A DELICIOUS VARIATION OF FRENCH DRESSING MAY BE MADE BY ADDING THE FOLLOWING INGREDIENTS TO THE ABOVE RECIPE.

¼ TEASPOON GARLIC SALT
½ TEASPOON CELERY SALT
½ CUP TOMATO SOUP

BEAT ALL TOGETHER AND BLEND.

THIS RECIPE SERVES 12.

238.

ROQUEFORT CHEESE WHIP

1 CUP COTTAGE CHEESE
1/2 CUP MAYONNAISE
1/4 CUP GRATED ROQUEFORT
CHEESE

1. PLACE THESE INGREDIENTS IN A BOWL AND WHIP WITH AN ELECTRIC BEATER.

THIS IS AN EXCELLENT DRESSING FOR HEAD LETTUCE SALAD OR MAY BE USED FOR A POTATO CHIP DIP.

WHIPPED CREAM DRESSING

2 CUPS STIFFLY WHIPPED
CREAM
1 CUP MAYONNAISE

1. FOLD MAYONNAISE INTO WHIPPED CREAM.

THE USE OF AN EXCELLENT PREPARED MAYONNAISE WILL DETERMINE THE TASTE OF THE SALAD DRESSING.

239.

240.

NOTES

241.

INDEX

242.

243.

244.